PERSPECTIVES AND PATTERNS

Discourses on History

Among numerous other works,
Warren B. Walsh is the author of:

The Development of Western Civilization, 1940

Readers' Guide to Russia, 1945

Russia under Tsars and Commissars, 1946

Readings in Russian History, 1948

Russia and the Soviet Union: A Modern History, 1958

PERSPECTIVES AND PATTERNS

Discourses on History

WARREN B. WALSH

1962
SYRACUSE UNIVERSITY PRESS

Library of Congress Catalog Card: 62-16382

Manufactured in the United States of America
by the Vail-Ballou Press, Inc., Binghamton, N.Y.

TO ALL WHO HAVE GIVEN ME

OF THEIR KNOWLEDGE,

THEIR WISDOM, AND

THEIR UNDERSTANDING

Preface

After many years of looking at trees and grubbing among the undergrowth there arises an urge to try to see the forest in which one has labored. History, and subjects related to history, have been my major field of study for thirty-five years. The teaching of history has been my profession for twenty-eight years; supplemented by intermittent experiences in other fields, and enriched for me by associations with those who professed other subjects and followed different occupations. It has been an unanticipated dividend in writing these essays to find that I have learned more than I realized, though less than I should, from these experiences and associations.

The goal of the essays is modest. I lack the vision and the erudition required for a grand survey of history as a whole, and do not find, in what little I know, support for elaborate systems of meaning nor great designs. The abstract profundities of the philosophers of history are beyond my capabilities, and I confess frequent difficulty in trying to relate what they have said to the subject with which I have been so long concerned.

But, like most practicing historians, I have developed certain hypotheses and have reached some tentative conclusions. These are here set forth for the consideration and, hopefully, for the possible use of others.

The plan of the volume is as follows. The four essays are interrelated, but each is independent of the others and may be read separately. Points discussed at length in any one essay are merely adverted to in the others, and this only when development of a theme requires it. Repetitions are thus reduced, but not eliminated. They are exploited by cross-references. The first and briefest essay, "Every Historian His Own Historicist," examines some of the points which often seem to be at issue between historians and those who speculate upon the nature of history as a whole, or who attempt to fit history into some preconceived *schema*, or who seek to analyze historical knowledge and the methods of historians. The second essay, "Cheney's 'Laws' Reconsidered," uses Professor Edward P. Cheney's "six laws" as a vehicle for the discussion of the general problem of law in history. "Is History a Science?" reviews some of the arguments and tries to take a fresh look at a problem which keeps popping up no matter how often it is "settled." This essay also introduces the concept of the reality world, and seeks to demonstrate one use of this concept as an analytical tool. The final essay presents my conclusions to date on the nature of such history as I know. Whatever novelty this essay may possess rests upon its application to history of several concepts adapted from studies in social psychology.

The footnotes are intended not as authorities to buttress my opinions, but primarily as acknowledgments to those whose ideas and words I have borrowed. The notes do not cover my total indebtedness for it is not feasible to attempt to name all from whom I learned by listening rather than by reading. Their number is large; their interests and talents, varied. I hope that they will not consider their anonymity in these pages as a symbol of ingratitude on my part because this would be the reverse of the fact.

If I cannot single out individuals, I can at least formally record my thanks to three universities with which I have been associated. Two of them, Tufts and Harvard, provided my training and my apprenticeship in the craft of history. The third, Syracuse, has enabled me to practice this craft for over a quarter of a century. It also granted me support and temporary relief from duties so that I might order my thoughts and present them in this form.

Syracuse, New York
21 December 1961

WARREN B. WALSH

Contents

I

Every Historian His Own Historicist

THE WORDS *history* and *historian* have been in general use so long that almost everyone finds them familiar and assumes, as a matter of course, that he knows what they mean. There is no such familiarity nor self-assurance about the terms *historicism* and *historicist*, partly because these are technical terms of limited usage and partly because they have been invested with a variety of meanings by those who have used them. The late Charles A. Beard once wrote that historicism, ". . . takes on all the implications of empiricism, positivism, and, if not materialism, at least that rationalism which limits history to its purely experiential aspects." This is perhaps less a definition than an indictment.

G. J. Renier has been more succinct and even less sympathetic. He has dismissed historicism as a sociological doctrine with which an historian is not concerned. J. W. N. Watkins added another element by referring to "marxist [*sic*] and other historicist sociologies"; and Karl R. Popper described historicism as, ". . . the doctrine that it is the task of the social sciences to propound historical prophecies." Popper has also called historicism, ". . . the relic of an ancient superstition . . . [and] a very important part of that philosophy which likes to call itself by the name of 'Scientific Socialism' or 'Marxism.' "[1]

If, as these scholars suggest, historicism is only an aspect or a function either of sociology or of "scientific socialism," why should the subject be of any interest to historians in general? A clue is supplied by an historian, Pieter Geyl, and by a philosopher, M. C. D'Arcy, S.J. Geyl has pointed out a linkage to one of

[1] Beard's statement appeared in his essay, "That Noble Dream," originally published in 1935. It may be conveniently found in Fritz Stern (ed.), *The Varieties of History* (New York: Meridian Books, 1956), pp. 314–28; p. 318. The other references are to: G. J. Renier, *History: Its Purpose and Method* (Boston: Beacon Press, 1950), p. 231; J. W. N. Watkins, "Historical Explanation in the Social Sciences," in Patrick Gardiner (ed.), *Theories of History* (Glencoe: The Free Press, 1959), pp. 503–14; p. 509; Karl R. Popper, "Prediction and Prophecy in the Social Sciences," in Gardiner, *op. cit.*, pp. 275–85; p. 276. Professor Gardiner's introductions to the two parts of his anthology ("Philosophies of History," which is concerned with speculation and systematizations, and "Recent Views Concerning Historical Knowledge and Explanation," dealing with analysis), pp. 3–8, 265–74, and his notes concerning each selection, constitute brief and convenient summaries.

the great historians—a linkage which many lesser historians may find surprising. Historicism, Geyl has written, is ". . . the term that came into use for the approach to history that was derived from . . . [Ranke's] examples."[2] Father D'Arcy proposed and used a set of meanings much broader and more inclusive than those given the terms by Beard, Renier, Popper, and others. Father D'Arcy made historicism a synonym for "philosophy of history"; and historicist a synonym for "philosopher of history." He recognized that most historians regard historicists, or philosophers of history, "who indulge in large patterns and groupings of the past" as *bêtes noires*, and poked gentle fun at historians by adding that they have always unconsciously envied "those who played at being philosophers," but that, "We are all of us in our unbuttoned moods philosophers of history." He was less gentle, however, when he charged most historians with being unaware "of their own serious predicament," and unable "to offer a well-considered and balanced defense of historical knowledge."[3]

Without admitting either of Father D'Arcy's charges nor subscribing to all of his opinions, I have borrowed his definitions of historicism and historicist

[2] Pieter Geyl, *Debates with Historians* (New York: Meridian Books, 1958), p. 21.

[3] M. C. D'Arcy, S.J. *The Meaning and Matter of History* (New York: Meridian Books, 1961), pp. 8, 9, 15, 67, 79–80.

for this essay. If the reader chooses, he may therefore substitute philosophy of history and philosopher of history, respectively, for historicism and historicist whenever these words appear on these pages. D'Arcy's usage not only substitutes words for phrases; it also permits subsuming specialized meanings under a broader label. There are some difficulties inherent in breadth. T. S. Brocon has warned that neither the historian nor the historicist has set definite limits to his field with the result that each has been inclined at times to accuse the other of poaching.[4]

A few scholars have won fame both as historians and as historicists; the most famous of such dualists (and intellectual duelists) are Arnold Toynbee and Pieter Geyl. Father D'Arcy's remarks concerning the attraction which historicism exerts upon historians are corroborated, among other ways, by many of the presidential addresses to the American Historical Association, as well as by numerous inaugural lectures delivered by appointees to Chairs in History in the British universities. Historians in general, however, shy away from historicism like crows from the sight of a gun. Although an historian may admit under pressure that history and historicism may impinge upon each other, or even go so far as to admit the relevance to history

[4] T. S. Brocon, "Herodotus and His Profession," *American Historical Review*, LIX, 4 (July, 1954), pp. 829–43; p. 853. Hereafter cited as *AHR*.

of some parts of historicism, ". . . he refuses," as Fritz Stern has noted, "to deal with it explicitly."

> Speaking to the British Academy, a few years ago, on "The Present State of Historical Studies," E. L. Woodward explained that he would not approach "the fundamental problem of the nature of historical knowledge. I am in good company if I evade a master problem of this kind, since nearly all English historians have evaded it."[5]

It is the purpose of this essay, whose title is an obvious paraphrase upon Carl Becker's famous *Everyman His Own Historian*, to explore some of the reasons why historians feel as most of them do about historicism, and to suggest that the feeling should, at least from time to time, be put aside.

The historians' aversion to historicism, using that term for the moment in its special meaning of a doctrine of sociology or of social science and also in the broader meaning of a philosophy of history, stems both from the historicist's general approach and from the language in which he often conceals his thoughts. The distinguished historian, Gaetano Salvemini, described the situation in the following self-deprecatory passage.

[5] Fritz Stern, *Varieties of History*, p. 14.

In discussing the problem of whether history and the social sciences are science, I renounce all pretensions to elevating myself above the humble ground of common sense to the lofty spheres of philosophy. Not that the desire to rise to such levels is lacking in me; I have simply not the capacity. At those altitudes the atmosphere is too rarified for my lungs and heart. In the writings of many philosophers of our day, in spite of every effort I understand not one single thing. Their works seem to me to be fog factories. They produce on my mind the effect of inverted filters: when I begin reading, my ideas are clear; but when I have finished they become so turbid that, if I ask these philosophers a question and they kindly condescend to answer, the immediate result of the answer is that I no longer understand my own question.[6]

[6] Gaetano Salvemini, *Historian and Scientist* (Cambridge: Harvard University Press, 1931), pp. 33–34. Having been inclined to attribute my puzzlement at most historicism exclusively to my own inadequacies, I was delighted and somewhat reassured by this admission, even though tongue-in-cheek, from one of the masters of the craft of historiography. It does not excuse my shortcomings, but it makes me feel that Professor Salvemini might have sympathized with my reaction to a volume recently published by a highly regarded historicist. After hours of wrestling with this work, described as "one of the most important studies of the uses of historical knowledge to appear in the twentieth century," I was forced to conclude sadly that (a) I

There are shining exceptions, but much of the philosophizing about history reminds me of a sentence once ascribed by a young woman reporter to a colleague of mine. He and I were engaged in writing our first book, and had withdrawn for the purpose to Martha's Vineyard. News was scarce on the island that summer so when word got about that two young historians were at work on an ambitious project the local paper despatched a reporter in search of the story. She interviewed my colleague about our purposes, our methods of collaboration, and the progress of our work. Then, presumably searching for human interest, she inquired as to what we did for recreation. My colleague was a little nonplussed, but he mentioned swimming and sailing. Pressed for more information and recalling that we sometimes tried to amuse our friends' children, he mumbled something about playing silly games. The young woman evidently felt that her readers expected more even from young instructors. When her story was published, my colleague was astounded to find himself quoted as saying, "For recreation, we swim, sail, and play little games we make up to amuse ourselves." The writings of some historicists seem to fall into the category of little games made up to amuse themselves.

---

could understand most of it only by a tedious line-by-line reading and re-reading, and (b) that when I did understand what the famous man had written I found it to be either commonplace, or useless for my purposes, or both.

Historicists in describing the subjectivity of historians often rest their case partly on the familiar fact that historians are frequently unable to agree. This is also true of historicists, many of whom spend great efforts in refuting what some other historicist has said about history or historians. In so doing, they sometimes seem to mistake their theories for facts. Philip Guedalla once remarked that history repeats itself and historians repeat each other. It is tempting to suggest as an additional clause, "and historicists argue with each other." There is, of course, no reason why they should not argue with each other, or with historians; but the argumentation does not always result in clarification of either historicism or history.

The antipathy of many historians to historicism, and to some historicists, is perhaps explicable in part by analogy. The approach to history and historians made by some historicists suggests time and motion studies. The historicist examines the materials of history and the methods of historians for the purpose of determining how well the methods enable the historian to comprehend and explain his subject. Since the historian is likely to feel, rightly or wrongly, that he has a greater familiarity with the materials and a greater expertness in handling them than any outsider, the report of the time and motion study is not likely to be well received. This effect is frequently accentuated by the historicist's use of what he thinks of as "that essential of disciplined thought, technical language." [7]

The historian is aware of the value of technical language, and has, in fact, developed some of his own.[8] He habitually uses certain terms in ways which are not as precise in meaning as properly employed technical terms, but which are peculiar to historiography. Some words have been borrowed or adapted from mathe-

[7] The phrase is borrowed from Robert K. Merton's article, "Now the Case *for* Sociology," which appeared in *The New York Times Magazine* of 16 July, 1961, pp. 14 ff. Professor Merton was replying to an article by Russell Kirk, "Is Social Science Scientific?" published in the same journal on 25 June, 1961, pp. 11 ff.

[8] Professor Isaiah Berlin in his essay, *Historical Inevitability* (London: Oxford University Press, 1954), pp.51–52, points to the special terminology of the sciences and the lack of such technical language in history as one of the key distinctions between the two. The historian, according to Berlin, generally employs only common concepts, and speech. There is less difference than might at first appear between this view and my comment. I agree that the historian generally uses everyday language. In fact, I would argue that the historian who does not do so makes a serious error which gravely weakens his contribution to knowledge by creating difficulties of communication. I am in full agreement with Professors Trevor-Roper, Allan Nevins, and others, who urge that it is a prime obligation of the historian to educate the laity. To do so, one must use—so far as such usage is consonant with accuracy—language familiar to the laity. Though I am not insensitive to the need for precision in the use of language, I am not convinced that precision, at least in historiography, is best achieved through use of "technical language."

matics and the sciences—*factors, functions, dynamics, evolution,* and the like; others, from the law—*bequeathed,* for example; or from the traditional languages of diplomacy. Many of the latter are foreign, reflecting a time when Latin, and, later, French were regularly employed in international communications. *Quid pro quo, status quo ante, casus belli, démarche, rapprochement,* and *entente* are familiar illustrations. The domination of a particular nation, and language, also leaves traces as in *Weltpolitik* and, more recently, *troika.* The historian takes such usages for granted, nor does he object to the employment of technical terms when these are appropriate, or necessary for precision. It is kidnaped or mongrelized or synthetic terms—such as *aimscales, social valences, social physics,* and *structuring a concept*—which seem to him to be jargon, use of which achieves obfuscation, rather than clarity or precision.

The real barrier between historian and historicist, however, is not semantic. It is, from the historian's viewpoint, that he and the historicist do not seem to be talking about the same problems. The historian frequently finds it difficult, and sometimes impossible, to recognize in the historicist's descriptions and analyses the craft which the historian thinks he practices. The two, to borrow an expression from a third field, are not operating on the same wave length. Points which, judging from the amount of time and space spent on them, appear very significant to the historicist often seem to the historian to be irrelevant, or unimportant, or unrealistic, or too commonplace to warrant extended discussion. Sometimes they seem gratuitous.

Every historian knows, because it is an essential part of his daily business, that he normally operates not as an actual observer of nor participant in the occurrences and events which he seeks to describe. He must work at many removes therefrom, and he sees little value in verbose reminders of this. Most historians are continuously aware of their inescapable dependence upon others for information. They are also aware of the limitations which this places upon them. M. Louis Halphen expressed this very well.

> Where documents are mute, she [history] is mute; where they are overly simplified, she is overly simplified; where they give a false echo, she is deformed.[9]

Some historicists have been greatly concerned over the historians' inability, partly because of faulty sources and partly because no one has yet discovered how to travel backwards in time, to know all the past. No historian, not even Toynbee at his most grandiose, pretends to know all that has gone on in human affairs. Few persons, in fact, assume that they know all about

[9] *Introduction à L'Histoire* (Paris: Presses Universitaires de France, 1948), pp. 49–50.

even that part of current events which directly affects them. Why, then, make an issue about inability to know all about past happenings? Why argue, as some have, that ignorance of the total past proves ignorance of any part of it; or that ignorance of all of a segment of the past shows an inability to know any bit of it? Is imperfect knowledge always so dangerous that no knowledge is preferable? Should those physicists who are now probing very uncertainly into ion propulsion and the magnetic tides of space cease their efforts because their observations are incomplete and may be inaccurate? They presumably find the unknown challenging, and a continuous reminder that their findings are tentative. Most historians feel the same way, and do not understand the strictures of the historicists on this point.

The preoccupation of some historicists with "laws," whose discovery they confidently anticipate and by virtue of which they hope to be able to predict human behavior, does not seem to most historians relevant to the problems of historiography. The obvious exceptions are those historians who operate within the framework of some deterministic theory. Historiography for Communists is a tool of politics, a weapon in the class struggle, an instrument for the "correct education" of the masses. Nor have the Communists been the only ones to abuse history for their own purposes. Historiography has been perverted to the service of racism, nationalism, fascism, partisan politics, and organized religious groups. No nation, no group, and no period have been free from such perversions; reason enough, it must be admitted, to account for some of the suspicions which are directed against historians and their craft. But this leads the discussion away from the broader subject of laws in history, and of the historicists' reactions to the historians' inability to find such laws. The issue is not the correctness of either position, but simply that historians, by and large, do not feel that the discovery or derivation of such laws is part of their business. Perhaps they should feel differently; that they generally don't, means that this is another instance when historians and historicists are either talking at cross purposes, or aren't communicating with each other.

Some historicists, by reason of their greater understanding of history, in the historians' sense, and their keener appreciation of what historians think their problems to be, are more meaningful and more helpful.[10]

[10] The inevitable omissions in a partial listing may be misleading but that risk is worth accepting if the list encourages students of history to make their own explorations.

Patrick Gardiner displays understanding and appreciation both in his monograph, *The Nature of Historical Explanation* (London: Oxford University Press, 1952) and in the editorial comments in his previously cited anthology, *Theories of History*.

Others who show like characteristics include: Isaiah Berlin, Morris R. Cohen, William Dray, Maurice Mandelbaum, Ernest

Even in their writings, there are occasions for misunderstandings and disagreements. Professor Mandelbaum, for example, making a case for the historian, wrote:

> Historical events are therefore observed, and not only are they observed they are in many instances also recorded by many men in many countries, and this is analagous to the repetition to which the events in the natural sciences are subjected. [Common observation and reporting add up to] . . . verification by repetition.[11]

In setting this up, Mandelbaum stated that an historian deals with events which are common property while a scientist deals with events observable in his own laboratory. Presumably what he meant was that the usual scientific experiments affect fewer persons

---

Nagel, Michael Scriven, and W. H. Walsh. Excerpts from the writings of all these gentlemen except Cohen may be conveniently found, along with many others, in *Theories of History*. For Cohen's views, see his article, "Causation and Its Application to History," *Journal of the History of Ideas*, 3 (1942), pp. 12–29; and his book, *The Meaning of Human History* (LaSalle, Illinois: Open Court Publishing Co., 1947). See, also, Mandelbaum, "Concerning Recent Trends in the Theory of Historiography," *Journal of the History of Ideas*, 16 (1955), pp. 506–17; and his book, *The Problem of Historical Knowledge: An Answer to Relativism* (New York: Liveright Publishing Corporation, 1938).

[11] Mandelbaum, *op. cit.*, p. 188.

and are known to fewer persons than are historical events. This is not certain. Some scientific experiments are known to many observers in considerable detail while in progress, the American astronaut shots being cases in point. Knowledge of many more experiments is shared after the event by publication, and/or by repetition of the experiment. There are also those scientific developments which occur independently and simultaneously, or nearly so; one example being American and Soviet work with masers (microwave amplification by stimulated emission of radiation). Although historical events, as opposed to lesser historical occurrences, can be considered common property in the sense that many persons know something about them, the sources concerning the events are not always common property in the sense of being available to any historian who may wish to examine them. The Soviet Union, for instance, possesses a large number of historical sources dealing with the work of the *zemstva*. These would be of great value to any historian interested in the last fifty years of the Russian Empire, but access to this material has so far been refused to American historians. The distinction which Mandelbaum sought to make thus seems unrealistic to an historian even though he may be grateful for the suggested analogy.

Professor Mandelbaum happens also to be one of the historicists who affirm that historians are competent to seek causes of historical occurrences and events. This is gratifying to an historian who finds himself constantly seeking answers to why and how, as well as to what. He can draw no comfort and little aid from those historicists who maintain that causation is beyond the historian's ken, being exclusively the preserve of the scientist. To the historian who argues that he is properly and actively concerned with causes, such historicists coldly reply that the historian is sadly mistaken in what he thinks to be causes. This does not leave much room for continued discussion. Neither do the views of historicists who perceive from within a theological reality world.[12]

Charles S. Leavenworth concluded, for example, that: "Human progress is evidence of Divine Providence. That is the greatest of all the lessons of history." John McIntyre intended his study ". . . to demonstrate that the Christian, because of his belief in God's Revelation of Himself in history, is committed to a unique doctrine of history. That this doctrine is not merely a theory concerning facts which are accepted by all men, but relates to the central nature of history itself." A distinguished president of the American Historical Association took as the subject of his presidential address, "The Christian Understanding of History," and he made it clear that by Christian he meant one who accepted the doctrines of the Trinity

[12] For a discussion of reality world, see the essay entitled, "Is History a Science?" pp. 90 ff.

and of the Resurrection of Christ. Spokesmen for the Roman Catholic position include Father D'Arcy, one of his works has already been cited; and Jacques Maritain, who wrote: "In one sense, the Kingdom of God has already come—in the form of the Church, or the Mystical body of Christ, which is, as we have seen, the Kingdom of the state of pilgrimage and crucifixion." [13] Such statements and the position they symbolize are, of course, congenial, and presumably useful to historians who share the particular reality world of the given historicist. Turning to the secular end of the scale, the same comment applies to historicists and historians who share other special reality worlds. This includes, as Professor Popper noted in the source quoted before, the Marxists and quasi-Marxists. It also covers, as Popper did not note in that particular instance, many non-Marxists. Peter Lavrov's *Historical Letters,* for example, have a greater appeal for those who think of sociology and history as having moral bases than for those who do not.[14]

The behavioral sciences, now enjoying an increasing vogue, have stimulated a hope among some historicists

[13] Charles S. Leavenworth, *The Lessons of History* (New Haven: Yale University Press, 1924), p. 98; John McIntyre, *The Christian Doctrine of History* (Edinburgh: Oliver and Boyd, 1957), p. 11; Kenneth S. Latourette, *AHR*, LIV, 2 (January, 1949), pp. 259–76; Jacques Maritain, *On the Philosophy of History,* edited by J. W. Edwards (New York: Scribners, 1957), p. 150.

[14] *Istoricheskiya pis'ma* was first published in 1868–69 while

and historians that the latter may find in behavioral science new concepts and new methods with which to enrich historiography. Professor L. Krieger, in a very erudite article, sought to show what historians can and should learn from the behavioral scientists. He concluded that historians must continue what they have been doing, that is, continue to retain and apply their knowledge of the "old fields of history"; and also add to their knowledge the "new fields of history," in order to interweave the new skills with the old. Professor David Potter discussed at greater length what historians can learn from the behavioral scientists, and *vice versa,* using the problem of the determination of national character as the vehicle of his discussion.[15] It was Professor Potter's contention that historians have been sadly lacking in precision; that they base their ". . . narrative upon an extraordinary mélange of unstated premises, random assumptions, untested hypotheses, and miscellaneous notions about the na-

---

Lavrov was in exile because of his alleged connection with Karakosov's attempt to murder Tsar Alexander II. Lavrov was a member of the Land and Liberty Party, the first organized political party in Russia—revolutionary, but not Marxist. The *Letters* are also available in a French translation by M. Goldsmith, *Pierre Lavroff: Lettres Historiques* (Paris, 1903).

[15] L. Krieger, "The Horizons of History," *AHR*, LXIII, 1 (October, 1957), pp. 62–74; David M. Potter, *People of Plenty: Economic Abundance and the American Character* (Chicago: University of Chicago Press, 1954), see especially the Introduction and Part I.

ture of man, the workings of society and the causation of historical change."; [16] are generally unaware of this conceptual weakness and have made no really serious attempt at overcoming it. As to national character, ". . . a major historical assumption and one that has colored the writing of a vast body of historical literature. . . . historians have done very little either to clarify or to validate this concept which they employ so freely." [17] It was Professor Potter's hope that the historian could gain from the behavioral sciences of psychology, sociology, and anthropology an improved methodological and conceptual foundation for the analysis of what he called the human factor in individuals and in society. It is possible to share a part of this hope without also sharing the view of Professor Ralph Linton, which Potter appeared to endorse: "It seems safe to say that the next few years will witness the emergence of a science of human behavior." [18]

Potter and Krieger are not the only historicists [19] to advocate that historians ought to seek help from col-

[16] Potter, *op. cit.*, p. x.

[17] Potter, *op. cit.*, p. 8.

[18] Potter, *op. cit.*, p. xiv. Linton's prophecy was made in 1943. The reader of these essays will become aware that I am not averse to attempting to apply to history methods and concepts borrowed from other fields. I have grave doubts, however, about anything called a science of human behavior unless one means by "science" the systematic effort to ascertain facts and their interrelations.

[19] The designation is used only in reference to the cited works.

leagues in other fields, nor to call attention to the imprecisions of which historians have been guilty. It could be argued that a search for assistance among the behavioral scientists is only an outgrowth of the earlier turning for help to the physical and life scientists. It could also be suggested that the behavioral sciences are not as precise in concepts, assumptions, hypotheses, and methods as their proponents claim. To follow either the argument or the suggestion would extend this essay beyond its intended scope and purpose. It is sufficient to note that there are almost as many varieties of historicism as of history, and that it behooves the historian to explore widely before abandoning the task as profitless.

The historians' usual first impressions—that either the historicists have nothing to say to historians, or that they are intent only on increasing the historians' difficulties—need revision. These impressions are true of some historicists, but not of all of them. There are those whose concern is genuinely friendly, and whose desire to clarify problems and to assist in solving them is earnest. Such historicists can render valuable services to the craft of history if historians will permit them to do so. Part of the services consist in reminding historians of what we habitually do, or fail to do; in alerting us to our carelessness in thought and our looseness in language; in sensitizing us to actual and potential errors of commission and omission; and in suggesting to us ways of becoming more effective in practicing what we profess. There are also further values to be derived from some historicism.

Because most historians are as suspicious of mysticism as of historicism they would probably shy away from the following statement by Chief Justice Holmes.

> Life is a roar of bargain and battle, but in the very heart of it there rises a mystic spiritual tone that gives meaning to the whole. It transmutes the dull details into romance. It reminds us that our only but wholly adequate significance is as parts of the unimaginable whole. It suggests that even while we think that we are egotists we are living to ends outside ourselves.[20]

It is not possible, however, for a man to spend his professional life as an historian without developing a personal philosophy of history. It will not, probably, be conscious, nor systematically constructed. Its possessor, if charged with having it, will often deny possession. This is not necessarily bad faith nor self-deception; it is more likely a lack of awareness, or diffidence in dignifying what seem to be commonplace, disordered thoughts and impressions with the label of "philosophy." To claim so grand a title for a random collection of assumptions and opinions may seem os-

[20] Quoted in "Holmesian Opinions," compiled by E. F. Murphy, *The New York Times Magazine*, 5 March, 1961, p. 80.

tentatious. There is no need to insist on terms. What matters is that a scholar cannot deal with human actions and human affairs day in and day out, both as scholar and as man, without accumulating some notions as to why men behave as they do.

The notions may be ill-founded, or unfounded; the projections of a too limited experience. They may be inaccurate analogies for the situations to which they are applied. They may be too vague, or too loosely formulated—like the concepts of national character or of public opinion. What does the historian mean by public opinion? Is it to be found in the editorial columns? Letters to the editor? The writings and speeches of public figures? Election returns? Reported interviews with chance-met, chance-selected "men in the street"? The comments of one's associates? Historians have used the term to mean all of these, and more; often without asking such elementary questions as whether editorials, for example, are intended to reflect or to form the opinions of others. In this instance, and in others, historians are too often content, as Professor Berlin noted, to use without examination popular concepts and categorizations. This is not a plea for the adoption of pseudoscientific concepts or a terminology which may give the appearance but cannot produce the fact of precision. It is a suggestion that the systematic evaluation of our accumulated notions might make us better historians.

Finally, there is the view so well expressed by the British historian, Trevor-Roper, in the course of his discussion of historicism. After expressing doubts about historicism in general and especially about laws in history which, he said, if discovered, would reduce history to engineering, he concluded as follows:

> Nevertheless, I believe that a man who undertakes to profess even some scattered parts of a great subject ought at some time to have considered the whole of it and should be prepared on some occasion to express his thoughts.[21]

The goal may be much more modest than considering the whole of history, a task far too ambitious for most of us to attempt, but even we may aspire to consider history in terms wider than our particular areas of concentration. We might, for example, limit ourselves to the retesting of some of the assumptions and concepts we have long taken for granted, or attempt systematically to organize and evaluate thoughts and impressions gathered over the years. We have small ground for complaint about historicism if, by default, we leave it to the historicists to think about the subject which we profess. This does not mean ignoring nor rejecting out of hand the suggestions and criticisms

[21] Hugh R. Trevor-Roper, *History Professional and Lay* (London: Oxford University Press, 1957), p. 4. The occasion was his inaugural lecture at Oxford.

of the historicists. Neither does it mean that the historian should seek from the historicists authorization for his opinions. The essence of the exercise, whether one chooses to look at all of history or only at some part of it, is that the opinions one finally achieves shall be one's own. It is in this sense that every historian should become his own historicist.

II

Cheney's "Laws" Reconsidered

Over a generation ago the late Professor Edward P. Cheney addressed the American Historical Association on "Law in History." [1] His theme was that neither individuals nor groups nor chance but "some inexorable necessity" controlled human affairs. "So arises," said Cheney, "the conception of *law in history*. History, the great course of human affairs . . . has been subject to law." Despite a contemporary's characterization of the address as significant and "an important event in American historical scholarship," there is little in the published record to indicate that Professor Cheney's thesis earned much

[1] The occasion was Cheney's presidential address before the annual meeting of the Association on 27 December, 1923. The address was originally published in the *American Historical Review*, XXIX, 2 (January, 1924), pp. 231–48. It was later republished by Professor Cheney in *Law in History and Other Essays* (New York: Knopf, 1927). My references are to the cited volume of the *Review*, hereafter indicated in this essay as *AHR*, XXIX, 2. The italics are in the original.

acceptance in the profession.[2] Nor, to judge again from the printed record, did it attract more than passing attention.[3] Classroom and other discussions of Cheney's ideas were presumably more numerous.

Four features of the essay are salient. First, despite a disclaimer of certainty, Professor Cheney's whole

[2] Frederick J. Teggart, *Theory and Processes in History* (Berkeley: University of California Press, 1960), pp. 204, 207. This is a second printing of a republication (1941) in one volume of two books which were originally published by the Yale University Press: *The Processes of History* (1918) and *Theory of History* (1925).

[3] There is, for example, no mention of Cheney in such studies as the following, although references to and quotations from Beard, Becker, Robinson, Teggart, and other of Cheney's contemporaries are common: Pieter Geyl, *Debates with Historians* (New York: Meridian Books, 1958); M. C. D'Arcy, S.J., *The Meaning and Matter of History* (New York: Meridian Books, 1961); G. P. Gooch, *History and Historians of the Nineteenth Century* (rev. ed., Boston: Beacon Press, 1959); Fritz Stern (ed.), *The Varieties of History* (New York: Meridian Books, 1956); G. J. Renier, *History: Its Purpose and Method* (Boston: Beacon Press, 1950); and Patrick Gardiner, *The Nature of Historical Explanation* (London: Oxford University Press, 1952) and (ed.) *Theories of History* (Glencoe: The Free Press, 1959).

J. G. Randall mentioned Cheney's, "Law in History" in his presidential address to the AHA in 1952. J. G. Randall, "Historianship," *AHR*, LVIII, 2 (January, 1953), pp. 249–64. This is the most recent reference I chanced to note, but I may have overlooked others because my purpose was not to establish definitively the number of published references to Cheney's

approach gives the impression of dogmatic certainty. This may have been due to an effort to state his ideas strongly and vividly in order to compel attention, but the apparent dogmatism is unattractive and may have repelled readers and hearers. Second, Cheney's claims were far too sweeping. Some must be rejected; others, substantially modified. Third, historical relativists will readily find in Cheney's essay "proof" of their contentions about historians' inescapable subjectivity. In fact, one need not be an historical relativist to recognize in Cheney's thinking some clear reflections of the hopes and fears of his time. Fourth, some of Cheney's ideas on "laws in history" merit serious reconsideration today. These four features will be considered in order.

Professor Cheney began his essay by citing half a dozen historical events which he believed demonstrated "a certain inevitableness . . . some inexorable necessity controlling the progress of human affairs." He then went on to declare:

---

essay (or address). It suffices my purposes to note that such references have been infrequent, and to deduce from this that the essay apparently had only a limited and passing impact upon either historians or, to borrow Father D'Arcy's terminology, historicists.

My first acquaintance with Cheney's "Law in History" came in an undergraduate course taught by Dr. Halford L. Hoskins in 1929–30. The general recollection of it lingered hauntingly in the back of my mind for thirty years before I found an opportunity to renew the acquaintanceship.

> If a thousand instances were taken instead of five or six, all would show the same result. Examined closely, weighed and measured carefully, set in true perspective, the personal, the casual, the individual influence in history sinks in significance, and great cyclic forces loom up. Events come of themselves, so to speak; that is, they come so consistently and unavoidably as to rule out as causes not only physical phenomena but voluntary human effort. So arises the conception of *law in history*. . . . This is an old conception. . . . Providence, fate, destiny, law, has controlled the affairs of men, as it controls all things.[4]

After elaborating this briefly, Cheney discussed the individual's subjection to physical, chemical, and biological law; added that men's minds are controlled by psychological and social laws; and concluded, "Man is simply a part of a law-controlled world." Turning to laws in history, and remarking that they "may be no more apparent than the laws that govern the wind and the storms," he inquired as to their nature. "Are they like objective statutes, or like the subjective laws of mathematics and logic, or like physical laws, or biological laws, or economic and moral laws? When we have found it [law in history] we shall know what it is like." He may have felt uncertain as to its nature, but he showed no uncertainty as to its existence: "Yet

[4] *AHR*, XXIX, 2, pp. 234–35.

laws in history there must be, and my guesses as to some of them are these." [5]

Reserving our consideration of his six "guesses" until later, we may finish the discussion of Cheney's certainty with his own words.

> May I repeat that I do not conceive of these generalizations as principles which it would be well for us to accept, or as ideals which we may hope to attain; but as *natural laws which we must accept whether we want to or not* [my italics], whose workings we cannot obviate, however much we may thwart them to our failure and disadvantage; laws to be accepted and reckoned with as much as the laws of gravitation, or of chemical affinity, or of organic evolution, or of human psychology.[6]

The sweeping character of Cheney's claims is already clear, but it becomes still clearer, and the need for revision becomes more apparent as we consider details of certain of his laws.[7] Cheney's second law he termed, interchangeably, "impermanence" or "mutability," and he applied it to institutions.

> So persistent and infinitely repeated has been this disappearance of successive organizations of

[5] *AHR*, XXIX, 2, p. 236.

[6] *AHR*, XXIX, 2, p. 245.

[7] The six laws were summarized by Cheney as follows: ". . . first, a law of continuity; second, a law of impermanence among

> men and types of civilization that it gives every indication of being the result of law rather than a mere succession of chances.[8]

This is likely to call to mind Toynbee's theory of challenge and response, but there is nothing in Cheney's essay to suggest that his thinking was running along that line. Cheney's thought turned to an analogy with what he called the biological law of the extinction of too highly specialized species, *e.g.*, the dinosaurs. He attributed the fall of civilizations to strict conservatism by which he meant the inability or unwillingness of the civilization, or organization, to change. "Unless nations can change as the times change, they must die." [9]

No one will quarrel with the observation that successive organizations of men have disappeared. The rise and fall of empires and nations have long intrigued the historian and the historicist, though neither has been able to agree either with the other or with his fellows as to the causes.[10] Historicists have been wont to twit historians on their inability to solve such prob-

---

nations; third, a law of the unity of the race, of interdependence among all its members; fourth, a law of democracy; fifth, a law of freedom; sixth, a law of moral progress."*AHR*, XXIX, 2, p. 245. We shall consider now the second, fourth, fifth, and sixth of these, reserving the first and third.

[8] *AHR*, XXIX, 2, p. 238.

[9] *AHR*, XXIX, 2, p. 239.

[10] "If we take the subject of the decline and fall of the Roman Empire, we have Gibbon attributing it to the triumph

lems. So have others who wish historians to produce not a record of what has been, but a "scientific" prediction of what is to be. Something of this latter thought was clearly in Cheney's mind as he worked out his "law in history."

> For practical uses, if history is to have a practical use, what we need is a clue to the future. This a knowledge of the laws of history might give us.[11]

This optimism, like his appeal to "biological law" for analogy, reflects—not surprisingly—Cheney's membership in his own time. He was a closer heir than are we to the optimism of the late eighteenth and nineteenth centuries, and his generation felt more

---

of religion and barbarism; Seeck attributes it to the destruction of the élite, Kaphen to physical degeneration, T. Frank to racial decline, Huntingdon to climatic conditions, such as the drying-up of the soil, M. Weber to the decline of slavery and the return to a natural economy, Rostovtzeff to a class struggle. Piganiol declares that this noble civilization was assassinated in the barbarian invasions, while Toynbee sees a failure of response to a challenge, the disaffection of the masses at a time of moral crisis." M. C. D'Arcy, S.J., *The Meaning and Matter of History*, p. 60. Father D'Arcy used the quoted passage to illustrate a point to which reference has been made and to which attention will be returned, namely, to borrow D'Arcy's words, "As we look back on past histories we see that they have been all in part conditioned by the outlook of their time and by the passions and prejudices of the particular authors."

[11] *AHR*, XXIX, 2, p. 247.

keenly than ours the impact of the Darwinian hypotheses. This is not to say that scholars, politicians, and others have ceased to demand, or to hope—depending upon their nature—that historians will be able to identify diagnostic signs of impending changes, nor that men have given up hope of progress. On the contrary, the whole Communist position, and not a little of their success, rests on their dogmatic conviction that their philosophy of history provides precisely such diagnostic signs. Nor have non-Communist historians and historicists ceased to look for analogies in the life sciences. A recent, moderate view has been put forth by Professor W. B. Gallie of Queen's University, Belfast.[12] It differs in its conclusions from Cheney's view, and also—interestingly—in its concept of conservatism.

Gallie holds that "all of our predictive generalizations" are necessarily based on a knowledge of history which is the indispensable ingredient of practical, "conservative" wisdom. "Conservative wisdom" he defines as a warning against "shortsighted opportunism—against the slick move that saves the day but ruins the cause." Gallie is quick to add that the conservatism he has in mind consists not of looking backward, but of a loyalty to inherited methods and principles, plus

[12] See W. B. Gallie, "Explanations in History and the Genetic Sciences," in Patrick Gardiner (ed.), *Theories of History*, pp. 385–402. The paraphrase which follows is from pp. 401–402.

a determination to apply these, when practical and relevant, to new problems.

The American historian, Professor Louis Gottschalk, and the British historian, Professor A. F. Pollard, may have had similar thoughts on this subject. The social importance of history, said Gottschalk, stems from the way historians think about persistent problems. The historian thinks of history as a genetic process: the study of how man got to be what man once was and now is. "This way of thinking is sometimes called *historical-mindedness*." Professor Pollard, writing prior to 1907, stated his view of this particular use of history in the following words.

> The idealist unrestrained by history compares the present with Utopia, the desert with a mirage, which he seeks to realize by shortcuts across 'the meagre, stale, forbidding ways of custom, law and statute;' and thus he becomes a revolutionary. The student of history compares the present with a real past, and by means of a valid comparison gains some perception of the conditions and chances of orderly progress.[13]

[13] Louis Gottschalk, "A Professor of History in a Quandary," *AHR*, LIX, 2 (January, 1954), pp. 273–86; pp. 276, 279. The italics are his. A. F. Pollard, *Factors in Modern History* (first edition, 1907; third edition, 1932; reprinted, Boston: Beacon Press, 1960), p. 2.

One might, perhaps, successfully paraphrase Pollard by saying that if "politics is the art of the possible," history is the guide to what is possible. This, however, is a far cry from Cheney's law of impermanence which exacts destruction as the penalty of violation. So are the statements by Pollard, written half a generation before "Law in History," and those by Gallie and Gottschalk, written a generation after the publication of Cheney's essay. Few would quarrel with Cheney's assumption that continuous change is the way of life. "Chance and change are busy ever/Men decay and ages move." [14]

If it were possible to dissociate the word *law* from the connotations built up around it by the sociologists and other social scientists; if it were possible to hold to the narrower definition of a phenomenon which appears to be ceaselessly recurrent, the word could be applied to social change, and the thought could be formulated acceptably in the generalization that all living persons and societies are constantly in flux as a necessary condition of life. But it will doubtlessly be argued that (a) such a statement is not really a law, being too vague and imprecise and (b) that to speak of living societies or organizations is naive anthropomorphism. Anyway, this more limited application is not what Cheney had in mind.

Cheney defined his "law of democracy" as "a tend-

[14] John Bowring, 1825.

ency for all government to come under the control of all the people." [15] He argued that democracy had proved its right to triumph by its greater legislative and administrative wisdom; and that better living standards, education, and moral training all combined "irresistibly" to extend it.[16] He was confident that the rise of dictatorships following the First World War "must be temporary," a reflection not only of the optimism noted earlier but also of a perhaps unrealized unwillingness to recognize that the expenditure of men and material had not made the world safe for democracy everywhere. It seems likely that Professor Cheney was not thinking of non-European nations nor of non-European labor—omissions which must be regarded as vitiating his law of democracy. But it should be recalled in extenuation of his position that new nations, democractic in form if not in fact, had been carved out of the old European autocracies. One could still think of Lenin's Russia as emerging from a temporary period of violence and terror into the New Economic Policy, which seemed to many non-Communists to presage a return to capitalism; and, at home in the United States, the labor movement was making gains. Would the events of the last forty years have caused Cheney to revise his thinking on this? One

[15] *AHR*, XXIX, 2, pp. 241, 242.

[16] Professor Cheney explicitly included "industrial democracy" along with "political democracy."

can only guess, but there is a hint of dubiety in the sentence with which he concluded this part of his discussion.

> If there is no such law [of democracy] we are adrift on a sea whose winds and tides and shores are all unknown.[17]

Did he enunciate a law of democracy because he found this alternative so inacceptable as to be emotionally unthinkable? An analagous situation led some prominent atomic scientists to assert during the later 1940's, and thereafter, that there simply had to be international control of atomic energy because the alternative was too horrible to contemplate. Both these scientists and Professor Cheney were perhaps too sanguine about man's ability and willingness to seize upon the rationally desirable choice.

Equally sweeping and equally reflective of what Professor Beard would presumably have called "the frame of reference in the mind of the selector," [18] are Cheney's "law of necessity for free consent," and

[17] *AHR*, XXIX, 2, p. 242.

[18] The phrase is quoted from C. A. Beard, "Written History as an Act of Faith," *AHR*, XXXIX, 2 (January, 1934), pp. 219–31; p. 227. See also Professor Samuel E. Morison's acid comments on this essay of Beard's in "Faith of an Historian," *AHR*, LVI, 2 (January, 1951), p. 261–75. Morison there refers to Beard's "frame of reference history" as the only kind that an historian can write under a dictatorship.

his "law of moral progress." As to the first, Cheney declared:

> Human beings are free agents . . . they cannot permanently be compelled. Not only should all government be by consent of the governed, but all government has been by consent of the governed. . . . It is consent, not force, that has on the whole held society together, that has supported governments, that has procured services. The consent has often been reluctant, it has never been actually forced. When forced it has not been consent, but mere yielding to violence, and violence has borne little fruit of achievement or permanence. . . . The law of free consent has doubtless been disregarded more than it has been obeyed, but it is none the less a law, violation of which has been followed by failure to obtain the advantages that conformity to it would have entailed. . . . the effects of force in history have been temporary, partial and illusory; voluntary acceptance alone has been permanent and adequate and substantial.[19]

Cheney obviously used permanent here in an institutional sense. A man who spends his entire life in slavery might certainly be considered to have been permanently enthralled and compelled. This cannot be what

[19] *AHR*, XXIX, 2, pp. 243–44.

Cheney had in mind. He must have been thinking in terms of a continuum of generations—son, father, grandfather, great-grandfather, great-great-grandfather, and so back to the beginning. A claim of permanence in this sense is irrefutable because the end of permanence does not seem to be finite. The full course has not yet been run. Perhaps, if the run is long enough, Cheney will be proved correct. No one can yet know. But Cheney's assertion reflects a hope, not a demonstrable fact. Nor is it possible to prove his further assertion that disregarding the law of free consent exacts the penalty of at least partial failure. Perhaps failure would have been greater under free consent. Difficulty of another sort also obtrudes on Cheney's fifth law.

How can the effects of voluntary acceptance be permanent if there is a law of the impermanence of nations? One could argue that Cheney implied the possibility of permanence for those nations which change as the times change. By permanence, in this case, he presumably meant continuity of an institution; that is, its continued existence despite changes in some aspects. But no reason is adduced to show that dictatorial governments are incapable of changing with the times, nor that governments which rest on the consent of the governed are bound to change. Confusion results when one tries to combine Cheney's insistence upon the persistent and infinitely repeated disappearances of organizations and civilizations with his later declaration that all government has been by the consent of the governed. This must mean that governments which rested on the consent of the governed—that is, upon voluntary acceptance—historically failed to change with the times and disappeared in consequence. If so, what are the grounds for arguing that voluntary acceptance, as opposed to involuntary acceptance, or yielding to violence, has been permanent?

The operation of the "law of moral progress" Cheney spoke of as being obscure and slow but visible and measurable. He believed that moral influences were growing stronger than material influences in human affairs, and he found evidence of this partly in the publicized causes of war. No nation, he said, would now go to war just for plunder or for revenge; "better" causes for war than the purely material have had to be offered. He adduced as further evidence of growing morality the abolition of slavery, a greater social conscience and justice, and the extension to relations between nations of principles once applied only on a much more limited scale.

> There was a time when fidelity to contract, justice, mercy, applied only within the family. The validity of these principles gradually extended from the family to the tribe, to the nation,

> and now in these later ages from the nation to international relations. . . . In moments of depression concerning international relations it may be a solace to consider how recently humanity has risen to a realization of its international duties, and yet how sure is its progress toward that realization, for it is a progress governed by law.[20]

Many of Cheney's professional contemporaries probably had reservations about the final clause, and it strains the credulity of those who have seen not one world war, but two, and who have watched one international contract after another broken. As these lines are typed, the threat of a nuclear war hangs over us. It becomes increasingly difficult to share Cheney's confidence in the sureness of "progress toward that realization." The strains and pressures of the day properly raise doubts, but a completely cynical disdain for Cheney's optimism is unwarranted. That moral progress is a natural law bound to come to pass in spite of what men may do seems most unlikely. That there has been progress along the lines Cheney indicated seems undeniable even though that progress has been varied, imperfect, and far from uniform. Men's value judgments have changed and are changing—not always for the better, but often so. Perhaps there is not

[20] *AHR*, XXIX, 2, p. 245.

a lesser willingness to accept social injustices than there used to be, but in many parts of the world men increasingly feel that there is a chance to correct social injustices. Neither the exceptions to this, nor a suspicion that efforts to eradicate some injustices often have been accompanied by greater evils, alters this fact. The guarantee of progress which Cheney apparently felt was implicit, may be invalid; the possibility of progress exists.

The four statements which have been discussed seemed to Cheney to be, as he put it, not generalizations nor ideals but "natural laws, which we must accept whether we want to or not." They certainly seem to a later generation, and probably seemed to many of Cheney's contemporaries, to be precisely the reverse. Part of the non-acceptance of Cheney's thesis may have been due, as has been suggested, to the rigidity of his presentation and to the all-inclusive nature of his claims. His insistence that his "laws of history" were in the same category as laws in the physical and life sciences left little room for compromise. His apparent take-it-as-is-or-not-at-all attitude did nothing to induce a partial acceptance. It may be supposed that all who were sure that history is not a science, or who rejected the notion of scientific law in history almost automatically took the second option. Others may have been repelled by a concept of immutable laws which reduced drastically the role of the individual.[21]

Both historians and historicists, but particularly the latter, have been much exercised over the question of whether history is a science. The literature on this is voluminous, and the arguments are as extensive as they are inconclusive at least partly because most writers find it necessary to define and redefine terms to their own liking. The extremes are easy to summarize. They range from Bury's dictum that ". . . history is a science, no less and no more . . ." to Swain's flat denial that history is a science in either purpose or method.[22] A more moderate position is possible if one defines science as comprising all efforts to ascer-

[21] Professor Cheney anticipated this objection and sought to meet it by saying that immutable law in history (or human affairs) left men with a freedom of action comparable to that, for example, of a chemist who must work within the laws of chemistry. "Law . . . does not bind thought or make man powerless, it only lays down the condition under which he must think and act. . . . Men have always been and are free to act; the results of their actions will depend on the conformity or nonconformity of these actions to historic law." *AHR*, XXIX, 2, pp. 246–47.

[22] Professor Bury's statement may be conveniently found in Fritz Stern, *Varieties of History*, p. 210. Professor Swain's denial appeared in a series of three articles under the title, "What Is History?" J. W. Swain in *The Journal of Philosophy*, vol. XX (1923), pp. 281–89, 312–27, 337–49; p. 348. It would be impractical to attempt to give here even a selected bibliography of the writings on this subject. Both bibliographies and some of the

tain facts and their interrelations,[23] and many have taken the compromise position that history is an academic discipline which uses scientific methods as much as possible, but is not a science. The decisive point for many is that a science is distinguished by its capability of discovering "universal relations between repeatable elements," that is, laws.[24] Cheney obviously thought that history shared this capability, thus putting himself beyond the pale, as it were, for all who disagreed. Yet there are certain observable social phenomena and human characteristics which, whether one chooses to call them laws, seem to be universally repetitious.

---

actual materials are readily at hand in the anthologies, already cited, prepared by Professors Stern and Gardiner.

[23] I have borrowed the phrasing from Gaetano Salvemini, *Historian and Scientist* (Cambridge: Harvard University Press, 1931), p. 3. This delightfully unpretentious little book is more profound than its easy readability (an unusual characteristic in this particular literature) might indicate.

My views on this problem are set forth in the next essay in this volume under the conventional title, "Is History a Science?" To avoid repetition, I will not discuss them here.

[24] The quoted phrase is from Morris R. Cohen, *The Meaning of Human History* (LaSalle, Illinois: Open Court Publishing Co., 1947), p. 36. There have, of course, been many other definitions. Compare, also, the entertaining article by Russell Kirk, "Is Social Science Scientific?" in *The New York Times Magazine* of 25 June, 1961; and the rejoinder by Robert K. Merton, "Now the Case *for* Sociology" in the July 16th issue of the same journal.

Two of these were set forth by Cheney in passages to which we now turn.

Cheney's first "law," which he described as being very familiar to historians, but comparatively new in historical writing and unfamiliar to laymen, is the "law of continuity." By this he meant something of the nature of *omnia vita e vita*, a view which, of course, does not attempt to answer the question of origins. Cheney handled it as follows.

> Actual origins elude us; everything is the outcome of something preceding; the immediate, sudden appearance of something, its creation by an individual or a group at some one moment of time, is unknown in history. . . . Institutions have been modified, not destroyed; races have been subjugated or absorbed, not exterminated; beliefs have altered, not ceased; human history has been an unbroken narrative. . . . The continuity of history is not merely a fact; it is a law. By no voluntary action can any great breach of historical continuity be accomplished.[25]

It is almost inevitable that the phrase, "the sudden appearance of something," currently calls at once to mind the sudden appearance in the heavens of man-made satellites. In one sense, Sputnik I was surely

[25] *AHR*, XXIX, 2, pp. 237–38. For the sake of emphasis, I have reversed the original order of the second and third statements.

something new, but it was not a discontinuity. On the contrary, and to take only one of very many possible illustrations, L. I. Sedov, called "Mr. Sputnik" by some of his Soviet scientific colleagues in tribute to his work on the first satellite, developed his skill in aerodynamics and aerodesign from his past training and experience in hydrodynamics and ship design.

This personal case exemplifies a broader characteristic which one finds repeatedly recurrent when examining the concept of "scientific breakthroughs," a phrase which has been given great currency in recent years by advertising writers. The major problem arises immediately when an effort is made to define the phrase. What constitutes a breakthrough? Who should be credited with having made it? Is the breakthrough made by the theoretical scientist who first suggests the possibility, or by the experimentalist who first demonstrates the possibility in his laboratory, or by the engineers and production men who first apply the scientist's findings? There is, for example, a device known as a maser (microwave amplification by stimulated emission of radiation) used, among other ways, as an extremely precise atomic clock for experiments testing the theory of relativity. Who made the breakthrough? Was it the American scientists who proposed the scheme in 1954, or the Soviet scientist who "invented" it in 1955 (these developments being independent of each other, so far as is known), or the Americans who built the first maser? A like case is the so-called

Cherenkov effect, named for the Soviet scientist who discovered this phenomenon in the 1930's. Did Cherenkov make the breakthrough, or was it those American scientists who developed this into a very sensitive tool for the measurement of high energy radiations? The identification of which particular discovery or advance is the real breakthrough is almost an impossibility. At the very least, it poses a question about which reasonable men honestly disagree simply because scientific discoveries and advances do not suddenly arise out of nowhere. Because of this fact, eminent scientists have expressed grave reservations about predictability in science. A typical conclusion is that of Edwin G. Boring, Emeritus Professor of Psychology at Harvard:

> It is true that the progress of thought is determined by psychological and social laws, and that we can often see after an event how it was predetermined by its antecedents. Specific prediction, nevertheless, almost always fails, or is right by mere chance, because the efficient antecedents are too numerous and too completely related to be correctly understood.[26]

The concept that history is an unbroken narrative, as Cheney phrased it, or a seamless web, or a contin-

[26] Edwin G. Boring, "Science and the Meaning of Its History," *The Key Reporter*, XXIV, 1 (July, 1959), p. 2.

uous existence rather than a series of unrelated though fortuitously associated events, to borrow Cohen's words, has been taken by some as the basis for attacking the objectivity of historians. The argument is that violence to truth is inescapable whenever one attempts to remove a segment for examination, and the length of the narrative makes such action imperative because no man could comprehend the whole.[27] What matters at the moment are not the relativists' attacks but their acceptance of the concept of continuity since their views render this recognition rather in the nature of an admission by hostile witnesses. Professor Morris Cohen, whose general position was different, once remarked that "Science and sanity postulate a world in which there are certain fixed characters." [28] The context, to a slight degree, and Cohen's other writing on the same subject, to a greater degree, encourage the inference that continuity in history was one of the fixed characters to which he referred.[29] It is striking that even

[27] Beard was one of the historical relativists who adhered to this view. For a helpful discussion of the problem see Ernest Nagel, "Some Issues in the Logic of Historical Analysis" in Gardiner (ed.), *Theories of History*, pp. 373 ff., especially pp. 378–79.

[28] Morris R. Cohen, "Causation and Its Application to History," *Journal of the History of Ideas*, 3 (1942), pp. 12–29; p. 23.

[29] Cohen warned, however, that ". . . the simple repeatable patterns of physics or physical laws have not been discovered in human affairs." Cohen, *Meaning of Human History*, p. 116.

so sweeping a series of changes as the Bolshevik Revolution necessarily left many aspects of life unchanged. Attention is so often concentrated on the large rather than the small, on the spectacular rather than the routine, on events as distinct from occurrences, that the extent of continuity is sometimes unremarked.

Cheney's "third law" was the "law of the unity of the [human] race, of interdependence among all its members."

> The human race seems to be essentially an organism, a unit. . . . No part of the human race in history has really progressed by the injury of another. . . . For I am not contending that human interdependence is an aspiration, a hope of the idealist; but that it is a law, to which the realist is just as subject as the idealist, inexorable in its workings, beyond our control, immanent in the conditions to which mankind has been and is subject.[30]

Objections to Cheney's reference to the human race as an organism may be admitted without prejudice to the whole because that reference is not essential to the concept of interdependence. It may also be agreed that Cheney was stating a truism rather than enunciating a law, provided it is recognized that truisms would not be so termed if they did not contain some

[30] *AHR*, XXIX, 2, pp. 240–41, 245.

element of truth. Professor Michael Scriven has stated this more formally.

> Historical explanations are secure against the depredations of future scientific discoveries just as much as scientific explanations are, law-based or not. The reason is that they are based on extremely reliable knowledge of behavior, despite its being usually too well known to be worth mentioning, and too complex to permit any precise formulation. It is a central error to suppose with Hempel that scientific laws are either more accurate or more useful than truisms as grounds for historical explanations.[31]

The recollection of Donne's often quoted lines suggests that not only have historians had no monopoly upon such insights, but also that they have sometimes been very slow to apply the insights of those outside the craft. It should be easier, not harder, for men whose world is being so rapidly shrunken by ultra high speed communications and transportation—not to mention globe-circling cosmonauts and radioactive fallout—to

[31] Michael Scriven, "Truisms as the Grounds for Historical Explanations," Gardiner (ed.), *Theories of History*, pp. 443–75; p. 471. Professor Salvemini refers to the laws which social science seeks to formulate as differing from proverbs only in greater sophistication and discrimination. Salvemini, *Historian and Scientist*, p. 137.

grasp the points made by Cheney. And, in fact, the growing concern of the two Very Great Powers and their associates over the underdeveloped regions and peoples argue strongly that there is an increasing though still imperfect appreciation of human oneness and interdependence. It does indeed seem as if an awareness of what is immanent in the conditions to which mankind is subject is being thrust more fully upon us all.

If it is argued, as it may well be, that this view again corroborates the claims of historical relativists and others who hold that historians, if not history, are inescapably subjective, so be it. Historians are always in some manner and in some degree subjective.[32] Whether they are more so than physical scientists is irrelevant to this essay. It may be accurate to remark that each generation must rewrite history for itself,

[32] Professor Geyl has called attention to the great Ranke's subjectivity which Geyl described as ". . . a dualism of labile historical and immutable moral standards." Pieter Geyl, *Debates with Historians,* pp. 9–29, especially pp. 16, 24. Geyl supported this interpretation by the following quotation from a letter of Ranke to his brother: "God lives and is observable in the whole of history. Every deed bears witness of him [*sic*], every moment proclaims His [*sic*] name, but especially do we find it in the connecting line that runs through history." This does not square with conventional interpretation of Ranke as the one historian whose unfailing detachment from the events he described enabled him to escape subjectivity.

but it is inaccurate to assert that such rewriting is always and in all cases motivated and controlled by economic or other determinisms. Sir Isaiah Berlin has cogently observed that a thesis which holds that men have to act as they do because of uncontrollable, external forces or conditions is an "historical alibi," and that if determinism is true, it dissolves the notion of human responsibility.[33]

Historians may rewrite history, as did the Beards, to advance some special cause or interest; but an historian may also make the attempt at rewriting because he believes that he has acquired new data, or new analytical tools, or new insights, or all three. In this he does not seem to differ substantially from, say, the high energy nuclear physicist who finds it necessary to rewrite physics because the mathematicians have provided him with a more powerful tool or because a new cyclotron of increased voltage permits more intensive (or extensive) experimentation. American and other space probes are currently requiring an almost continuing revision of astrophysics not only because of the discovery of new "facts," such as increasingly more accurate measurements of the Van Allen radiation belts, but also because these discoveries permit new insights and suggest new hypotheses.

[33] Isaiah Berlin, *Historical Inevitability* (London: Oxford University Press, 1954), pp. 33, 67. The whole of Professor Berlin's essay is highly pertinent.

Scholars habitually revise, reinterpret, rewrite as their learning or wisdom increases, and this applies whether they are physical scientists or historians. They may learn the wrong things, or they may draw erroneous conclusions, but what they think they have learned affects what they do next. The remembrance of how things were, or were thought to have been, provides what is usually assumed to be a partial foresight; not a certainty, but a sort of "best bet" based on past experience. This not only affects rewriting, but is also highly relevant to the problem of predictability in human affairs. There is, to use a common engineering term, an element of feedback on the basis of which modifications are often made. As Professor Cohen once remarked in a slightly different context, "men's views of what is happening are . . . causes of what happens." [34] This human characteristic, rather than

[34] Morris R. Cohen, *Meaning of Human History*, p. 119. Professor Karl R. Popper makes the same point succinctly and cogently in reference to predictability. Unlike Father D'Arcy, who equates historicism with "philosophy of history," and who describes an historicist as a philosopher of history (which is the way these terms have been used in this essay) Popper equates historicism with the assumption that historical prediction is the aim of social science, and this aim can be attained by discovering the "laws, rhythms, patterns, trends" of history. Popper maintains that the impossibility of predicting the future growth of knowledge makes it also impossible to predict the future course of history because the growth of human knowledge

any mystique about relativism or determinism, accounts in considerable part for the feeling of each generation that it needs a "new history."

There is, in short, something to be learned—both directly and through the stimulation of disagreement —from Professor Cheney's "Law in History." His chosen term of reference—that historical laws are identical in force and character to physical and natural laws such as the law of gravitation, to use his own example—is unacceptable if taken literally, and it appears that he meant it to be taken literally. It appears also that Cheney equated natural law with instincts or natural processes inherent in men and things, and rejected the less rigid view that even natural law may be subject to some uncertainties and should therefore be regarded as an intellectual concept or generaliza-

---

strongly influences what happens thereafter. Karl R. Popper, *The Poverty of Historicism* (Boston: Beacon Press, 1957).

What Cohen, Popper, and others say about predictability seems to me to apply with equal force to the so-called rewriting of history.

The problem is treated from an entirely different but nonetheless wholly relevant view in F. P. Kilpatrick, *Recent Transactional Perceptual Research: A Summary* (ONR Report, Princeton University, 1 May, 1955), pp. 2–4; and also in Hadley Cantril and Charles H. Bumstead, *Reflections on the Human Venture* (New York: New York University Press, 1960), *passim et seriatim.*

tion which holds good under most but not under all circumstances. In other words, law in history was to Cheney not hypothetical but real. Although he commented that his laws might be disregarded temporarily, thus explaining by implication why they might sometimes appear to be inoperative, he held that the laws eventually caught up with those who disregarded them. Disregard for, or apparent evasion of the laws, was, in Cheney's view, illusory. Sooner or later, the piper had to be paid. This suggests an analogy with man-made law under which a violator must be caught in order to be punished, but this is an imperfect analogy because not all violators are caught, and not all who are caught are punished. Cheney did not mention this analogy; did not, in fact, follow up his own suggestion that law in history might resemble statute law, presumably because he regarded law in history as not man-made. His analogy with natural law is also imperfect. The law of gravitation, for example, cannot be disregarded for an indefinite period.

The substitution for Cheney's *law* of the less demanding concept of *postulate* makes it possible to salvage some of Cheney's points. It may be argued, on one side, that this substitution completely alters Cheney's thesis. An undemonstrable and not indubitable proposition, that is, a postulate, is clearly different from an order of phenomena which is invariable under the given conditions, that is, a law. It can be argued on the other side, however, that Cheney's choice of terms was as inaccurate as it was unfortunate; that what he did was to postulate, that is, formally to enunciate without proof, certain assumptions which he labeled laws. Even if this is sound, and not a mere playing with words, not all of Cheney's assumptions were sound. His assumptions ("laws") of democracy, freedom, and moral progress are, at least, not self-evident; and his concept of the impermanence of nations needs clarification if not revision.

It was part of Professor Cheney's intention to make history more "practical" by finding a clue to the future. "This a knowledge of the laws of history might give us." [35] Many social scientists, though fewer historians, have shared this aspiration and this confidence in "laws." It is more fruitful to use insights such as Professor Cheney's as clues to a better understanding of the past.

[35] *AHR*, XXIX, 2, p. 247.

III

Is History a Science?

THE DESIRE to fit history neatly into a file labeled either SCIENCE *or* NON-SCIENCE, with appropriate subtitles, has long been endemic among professional and lay historians and philosophers of history, as well as others. Giambattista Vico, writing early in the eighteenth century on the nature of history, called it the new science, which could teach men to anticipate the endless recurrence of successive stages. Kant regarded all human history as "the realization of a hidden plan of nature," and thought it possible for philosophers to assist nature by working out the universal history of the world according to this plan. Herder believed that human powers activate history within limits set by God-given laws of growth and decay. Condorcet, who saw the past as the slow progress of men out of barbarism, thought that this progress was governed by universal laws which man could discover. Comte believed in human progress both as a present fact and as a continuing possibility, and he urged that there is a science of society of which history forms a part. J. S. Mill thought of history as the uncovering of those "empirical laws" which govern the stages of social growth, and of those "principles of human nature" from which the empirical laws are derived. Buckle, whose span of activity was approximately contemporary with those of Comte and Mill, shared their belief in laws which control human affairs and in the necessity for scientific history.

There are also distinguished thinkers on the "non-science" side. Although Hegel thought of history as moving toward the attainment of certain goals, he drew a clear line between the subject matter of history and natural science. Spengler, who was interested in working out a grand plan, took the position that the methods of natural science were inapplicable to history. Dilthey and Croce argued along similar lines; Dilthey maintaining that history could be comprehended only through a process which has been called "Dilthey's 'doctrine of understanding' " and Croce suggesting that the work of the historian was closer to that of the artist than that of the scientist. Collingwood, Croce's British disciple, was, however, sure that history was a science because history asked questions.

It is unnecessary to continue this review to make the point that speculation on the nature of history, and especially on its relation to science, has been going on for two and a half centuries. Some have traced its origin to the impingement of the physical sciences on traditional beliefs and ways of thought, an impingement which was apparent as early as the seventeenth century. Others have seen in it the continuing impact on thought of the great seventeenth and eighteenth century philosophers; and still others have held it to be a function of the development of historical criticism in the nineteenth century. The advances achieved by the new methods of historical investigation; the patent advantages of the new methods over the old, and the employment of what Langlois and Seignebos referred to as the "ancillary sciences," such as epigraphy and paleography, led some to believe that history had become, or was becoming, fully scientific. A less charitable suggestion has been that historians, wishing to share the prestige accorded to the physical scientists, have insisted that history is also a science. Interest in the nature of history has been persistent, and the speculation about the relationship of history and science has been wide-ranging and varied.[1] There are, however, undertones in this debate which recall the

[1] This essay will not attempt to list, let alone to discuss all the various "isms" which have been developed. It is manifestly impossible when so much has been written by so many to avoid retreading well-trodden paths, but one can try to avoid stepping in every footprint.

For a scholarly review of the thinking about history from ancient days to the late 1880's, see Pasquale Villari (L. Villari, tr.), *Studies: Historical and Critical* (London: T. Fisher Unwin, 1907). For an early review by an American scholar, see Frederick

arguments of graduate school days as to whether it required more work to earn a Ph.D. or an LL.B. Those arguments were always inconclusive. So, probably, is this debate, which some have sought to end by use of some such formula as: History—scientific in method, humanistic in content.

Namier, whose general view, "History is therefore necessarily subjective and individual, conditioned by the interest and vision of the historian," seems to embody something of Croce and Collingwood as well as of Beard and other relativists, has put forward the following solution.

> The discussion whether history is an art or a science seems futile; it is like medical diagnosis:

J. Teggart, *Prolegomena to History: The Relation of History to Literature, Philosophy, and Science* ("University of California Publications in History," 4, 3, August 30, 1916), pp. 155–292 (Berkeley: University of California Press, 1916). An excellent introductory summary is W. S. Holt, "The Idea of Scientific History in America," *Journal of the History of Ideas,* I (1940), pp. 352–62. A further discussion, concerned mainly with U.S. history but containing a useful set of definitions and an extensive bibliography, appeared in: *Theory and Practice in Historical Study: A Report of the Committee on Historiography*. Bulletin 54 of the Social Science Research Council, 1946. Two recently published anthologies provide in convenient form both a wide variety of excerpts and useful editorial comments. They are: Patrick Gardiner (ed.), *Theories of History* (Glencoe: The Free Press, 1959); and Fritz Stern (ed.), *The Varieties of History* (New York: Meridian Books, 1956).

> a great deal of previous experience and knowledge, and the scientific approach of the trained mind, are required, yet the final conclusions (to be re-examined in the light of evidence) are intuitive: an art. The function of the historian is akin to that of the painter and not of the photographic camera. . . .[2]

Professor Cecily V. Wedgwood arrived at a similar conclusion.

> All sciences are devoted to the quest for truth; truth can neither be apprehended nor communicated without art. History therefore is an art, like all other sciences.[3]

Whether communication is an art or a science, it is increasingly recognized as a complex and difficult problem. Charles P. Snow has more than once lamented in print what he regards as the almost complete breakdown of communication between scientists and others.[4] Anyone who has had much occasion

[2] Lewis B. Namier, *Avenues of History* (New York: Macmillan, n.d.), p. 8.

[3] Cecily V. Wedgwood, *Truth and Opinion: Historical Essays* (New York: Macmillan, 1960), p. 96.

[4] Charles P. Snow, *Science and Government* (Cambridge: Harvard University Press, 1961); *The Two Cultures and the Scientific Revolution* (Cambridge: Cambridge University Press, 1959).

to deal with scientists from different scientific disciplines is familiar with the rising barriers which separate not only field from field but also one sub-field of a science from another. The emphasis currently placed on training young scientists and engineers in the writing of reports is a further case in point. Among historians, part of the revulsion from the "history-is-a-science" school of thought has arisen from a realization that the dust-dry, pedantic, "scientific monographs" remained largely unread. Historians were reduced to talking to each other; frequently, to talking to themselves—a situation which is eventually recognized as being both futile and frustrating.[5] There has been increasing agitation within the profession for historians to return to the virtues, but to avoid the faults and limitations, of such literary historians as, for example, Macaulay and Parkman. Professor Renier has given a forceful—some would say an extreme statement—of the requirement that historians must communicate.

> This much is certain: the man who has not communicated to his fellow human beings, by

[5] The situation of the unread historian recalls a response by the philosopher-politician, T. V. Smith, to an inquiry as to why Professor Smith, who had been strongly advocating that scholars of politics immerse themselves in practical politics, served only one term in Congress. Smith replied that he had been guilty of making an elementary mistake: he had neglected to get enough votes to be re-elected.

publication or by private circulation, a story of past events, whether a kinetic narrative or a static monograph, is not an historian.[6]

There is still some disputation as to whether history belongs with the social sciences, or with the humanities, or is *sui generis* and should properly be regarded as a bridge between the two. There are those, like Krieger and Popper, who urge that historians and social or behavioral scientists have much to learn from each other and should really get together more often. There are also those who advocate that historians take into account some of the methods and concepts of psychology, biology, physiology and psychoanalysis.[7]

[6] G. J. Renier, *History: Its Purpose and Method* (Boston: Beacon Press, 1950), p. 54.

[7] Teggart was advocating as early as 1910 that the historian should borrow the concepts of psychology and the methods of biology, with emphasis on the latter. F. J. Teggart, "The Circumstance or the Substance of History," *American Historical Review*, XV, 4 (July, 1910), pp. 709–19. Hereafter cited as *AHR*.

S. Ratner argued in 1941 that historians ought to broaden themselves and their craft by using the methods, the concepts, and the findings of psychoanalysis and psychology. S. Ratner, "The Historian's Approach to Psychology," *Journal of the History of Ideas*, 2 (1941), pp. 95–109.

See also, W. L. Langer's plea to historians to consider the psychological factors. Professor Langer placed his chief emphasis on psychoanalysis, and suggested that historians ought to consider the psychic mass effects of such historical events as the medieval plagues. He also mentioned cooperation with social psychology, but appeared to confine himself to the Freudian

There has even been an attempt to work psychiatry and psychology into the history of the Progressive Movement.[8] No move has yet been made, however, to combine university departments of psychology or psychiatry and history. Although history is in some institutions subsumed under the controversial title of social sciences, it would be astonishing to find history organizationally linked with either the physical or the life sciences except under the very general label of arts

---

school. W. L. Langer, "The Next Assignment," *AHR*, LXIII, 2 (January, 1958), pp. 283–304; p. 302.

[8] John C. Burnham, "Psychiatry, Psychology and the Progressive Movement," *American Quarterly*, XII, 4 (Winter, 1960), pp. 457–65. Mr. Burnham's hypothesis seems to be that psychiatry and psychoanalysis form one aspect of the Progressive Movement, because the psychiatrists and psychoanalysts of the period belonged, like those politicians who were associated with the movement, to the American middle class. The effort seems to me to mistake coincidence for correlation, if not for causation. *Cf.* the following statements in "Causation and Its Application to History," by Morris R. Cohen, *Journal of the History of Ideas*, 3 (1942), pp. 12–29; p. 15: "A correlation is an empirical or historical statement that in a certain proportion of instances two elements have occurred simultaneously or successively. A causal relationship asserts more than mere past coincidence. It affirms that there is some reason or ground why, whenever the antecedent occurs, the consequent must follow." Correlation may suggest causation, but does not automatically prove it. A specious correlation—as in the famous observation that for thirteen years there was an 87 per cent correlation between the death rate in the State of Hyderabad and membership in the International Machinists Union—may reach absurdity.

and sciences. The answer to the question, "Is history a science?" has been negative in terms of academic organization.

The genesis of the question can be understood in terms of the history of historiography and of the sciences. Interest in it has been kept alive by a variety of reasons including the central place held by a theory of history, "historical materialism," in what Communists call their science of society. Their claims to have transformed history into a science of the same nature and validity as chemistry or physics [9] have compelled continued consideration of the question by both protagonists and antagonists of these claims. The growing influence and increasing sanguineness of the behavioral scientists have encouraged some to attack history as unscientific, incapable of predictions, and therefore of slight value. This has stung some historians into making contrary assertions; others into re-examination of the whole problem.

The distinction, or the identity, between history and science have been sought in the subject matter, the

[9] For example: "By its discovery of the basic laws . . . Marxism raised the theory of the history of humanity to the level of a genuine science, capable of explaining both the character of any given society, and the evolution of society from one social structure to another," O. V. Kuusinen *et alii*, *Osnovy Marksizma-Leninizma* (Foundations of Marxism-Leninism) (Moscow, 1959), p. 4. English translation by U.S. Joint Publications Research Service, N.Y.C. JPRS: 3829. 9/Se/60.

terminology, and the methodology of the two. The argument *ad hominis*, that historians are inescapably involved in their treatment of history and are therefore always subjective, has been common; and has been variously identified as historical relativism or historical scepticism. Professor Charles A. Beard, for example, although admitting that the historian enjoyed "the help of the scientific method," was dogmatic in his insistence that history is subjective because it must be "thought about past actuality." [10] Collingwood was inclined to want to have it both ways: that history is a science confined to the study of human affairs, and that the historian actually participates in history. He meant by the latter statement that the historian reconstructs the past by rethinking the thought of the participants.[11] This ignores a key point: the occurrence or event took place independently of anyone's subseqent thought about it. The historian, as Professor

[10] Charles A. Beard, "Written History as an Act of Faith," *AHR*, XXXIX, 2 (January, 1934), pp. 219–31; pp. 219, 227.

[11] R. G. Collingwood (T. M. Knox, ed.), *The Idea of History* (Oxford: Clarendon Press, 1946). Collingwood has been accused of borrowing his ideas from Croce. See, *e.g.*, Patrick Gardiner, *Theories of History*, p. 249: ". . . many of Croce's ideas on history appear in Collingwood's book, expressed in a less mystical and more understandable form." Knox admitted the similarity to Croce's of many of Collingwood's ideas, but insisted that Collingwood had arrived at them independently.

Morris Cohen once observed, does not make the past; he makes findings about the past. An occurrence or an event, or the relationships of occurrences and events, are discovered by the historian; not created by him.[12] Croce wrote about the "inwardness" of history, by which phrase he apparently meant that the historian must "relive" the past in his imagination, and that historical reality consists of this imaginative "re-creation." Perhaps this view of Croce's explains his phrase which is often misquoted as "all history is contemporary history." What Croce actually wrote, as Professor S. E. Morison once pointed out, was:

> The practical requirements which underlie every historical judgment give to all history the character of 'contemporary history' because, however remote in time events there recounted may seem to be, the historian in reality refers to present needs and present situations wherein these events vibrate.[13]

[12] Morris R. Cohen, *The Meaning of Human History* (La-Salle, Illinois: Open Court Publishing Corporation, 1947), pp. 48–50.

Throughout this essay, occurrence is used to indicate a lesser happening than an event. An event comprises many occurrences.

[13] S. E. Morison, "Faith of An Historian," *AHR*, LVI, 2 (January, 1951), pp. 261–75. Croce's statement was quoted by Morison from *History as the Story of Liberty*.

It will be suggested later that this has relevance and reality, but not in the sense given by Croce and Collingwood.

Professor Joseph W. Swain's extreme version of historical relativism was that historians, the descendants of ancient mythmakers, are simply modern mythologists who are believed. The distinction between history and mythology, according to Swain, is in method, not in essence. The mythmaker may invent and embellish, but the historian must stick to the truth. Sticking to the truth, however, cannot make history into a science, nor historians into scientists. There are two processes in science: the collection of data and the formulation of general laws. History cannot be a science because the historian cannot perform the second process. Moreover, to continue to paraphrase Swain, whole generations of historians reflect the interests of their times. All history and all historians are therefore inescapably subjective. Swain illustrated his argument with selections from numerous historians of whom he said, ". . . in every case, their views were the results of their personal opinions . . . [and] their philosophies." "Each age," Swain concluded, "must create its own past as it creates its own present and future." [14] This is obviously hyperbole since it is mean-

[14] J. W. Swain, "What Is History?" *Journal of Philosophy*, XX (1923), pp. 281–89, 322–27, 337–49; pp. 281–84, 289, 312, 322, 349.

ingless if taken literally. Taken either way, it leaves Swain in the position of denying that the general past affects the general present while affirming that the historians' personal pasts effectively control their professional present, the alternative being to assume that personal opinions and philosophies are created *de novo*.

The argument that the historian must be subjective because he is always the prisoner of the present assumes that the physical scientist is free from the tyranny of time and circumstances and is therefore free from subjectivity. When science is called objective, wrote Christopher Blake, ". . . it is clear that a comparison with the subjective is being made, *i.e.* there is no vacuous contrast, yet it seems hard to imagine how any piece of scientific discourse could ever be regarded as subjective in any sense." [15] The final phrase rules out restriction to special usage and, unless "scientific discourse" is to be thought of as divorced from men, it follows, according to Blake, that no scientist can be regarded as being subjective. This is nonsense. A study of chemical affinities is undoubtedly less likely to involve the student emotionally than a study of human affinities, but it does not follow that there are no subjective elements in the work of the physical scientists. Personal characteristics and circumstances affect the

[15] Christopher Blake, "Can History Be Objective?" in Gardiner, *Theories of History*, pp. 329–43; p. 335.

scientist's choice of a problem, his method of approach to it, and his insistence on "just the facts." [16] Human errors occur in the design, manufacture, and operation of experimental equipment—as in the famous case when one stage in the study of atomic fission was delayed because the experimenters inadvertently reversed a small piece of the apparatus.

The same essay by Blake also contains a prime example of the assertion that the distinction between science and history rests partly on terminology, that of the physical sciences being far more specialized and precise than that of history. This is true in general, but the appearance of complete objectivity given thereby can be misleading. Blake offers as contrasting illustrations the two following sentences: "I say, it's quite warm in here," and "At point (x, y, z, t) the temperature is 300°A." [17] He labels the latter sentence "objective," noting that this may mean no more than that it is acceptable to those familiar with the terminology, but adding that ". . . it can also suggest to some . . . something spatially independent of the

[16] For a brief discussion of this problem by a psychologist, see: Anne Roe, "The Psychology of the Scientist," *Scientific Manpower, 1960. Papers of the Ninth Conference on Scientific Manpower. Symposium on Sociology and Psychology of Scientists. National Science Foundation.* (Washington: Government Printing Office, May, 1961), pp. 48–52. See also pp. 90 ff.

[17] Blake, *loc. cit.*, p. 337. See also the brief discussion on this point in the essay, "Every Historian His Own Historicist," p. 6.

speakers, and hence outside the range of their personal feelings." It may be outside the range of personal feelings, but 300°A is not inherent in the temperature at a given point. It is a measurement on an arbitrary scale, subjectively chosen by some person or persons. The subjective element is not removed; it is only reduced so that the special terminology does not result in complete objectivity though it may seem to.

A more impressive distinction, and one more commonly cited, is to point out that the historian cannot recreate the past in order to test his hypotheses about it; cannot verify what allegedly happened by use of the experimental method. This is so obviously true as to seem completely convincing to many. Historical occurrences and events are unique because they cannot be reproduced under any conditions, let alone under controlled conditions. If experimentation is thought to be of the essence of the scientific method, it follows that the historian cannot use the scientific method. A discipline which is not susceptible to the methods of science cannot be a science, or so it has seemed to many. Others reached the same conclusion through a different line of reasoning, as follows. One may not derive from a single instance a law of human behavior which would make scientific prediction possible. Hitler, for example, can commit suicide in his bunker (or elsewhere) only once. That Hitler chose death rather than face the results of defeat cannot be held to prove that every dictator has made or will make the same choice. The uniqueness of historical occurrences and events therefore, as Swain said, makes it impossible for the historian to qualify as a scientist by formulating general laws on the basis of collected data.

Some have carried this argument further by asserting that the admitted uniqueness of historical occurrences and events precluded causal analysis and the verification of hypotheses by historians. Others have countered by noting that historical occurrences, though unique, may have some commonalities. King John could sign the Magna Carta at Runnymede only once, but other monarchs could yield to the pressure of their nobles by making concessions. Professor Maurice Mandelbaum made a different attack. Dealing specifically with the opinions of those who hold that causation is exclusively scientific,[18] Mandelbaum

[18] Maurice Mandelbaum, "Causal Analysis in History," *Journal of the History of Ideas,* 3 (1942), pp. 30–50. See also his book, *The Problem of Historical Knowledge: An Answer to Relativism* (New York: Liveright Publishing Corporation, 1938).

Mandelbaum in this article accepts as his working definition of *cause* that given by H. W. B. Joseph in his *Introduction to Logic* (London: Oxford University Press, 1916): ". . . the cause of an event being a complete set of those events without which the event would not have occurred, or whose non-existence or non-occurrence would have made some difference to it," p. 401. William Dray denies in his book, *Laws and Explanation in History* (London: Oxford University Press, 1957), p. 111, that

noted, first, that these are opinions, not facts; and that the effort to confine causality to science ignores the use of causality in everyday life. He went on to say that laboratory and field experimentation are not the only forms of controlled observation; and, further, that the natural scientist, no less than the historian, interprets his observations. Interpretation is not subjective; ". . . facts demand an explanation that fits them." Verification of interpretations are circular both in science and in history; hypotheses are tested by the plausibility of the interpretations they produce. If the interpretation is plausible, its underlying hypotheses are judged accurate. Later scholars, equipped by virtue of greater knowledge with new tests of plausibility repeatedly re-examine the case thus providing a check not wholly unlike that achieved through repeated experimentation.

Professor G. M. Trevelyan seems to have had a similar thought in mind when he wrote:

> Because there are many historians, truth does slowly and partially emerge. . . . And so, by

---

historians use cause in this meaning. I do not agree with Mr. Dray. Neither can I agree with Mandelbaum's statement that causal analysis is the distinguishing mark between history and chronicles. *Loc. cit.*, p. 40. In the old Russian chronicles, for example, Divine displeasure is often given as the cause of events. Sound or not, this is still causal analysis.

> various processes conducted by historians of very different types, the wide margins of error and ignorance are reduced.[19]

The implication of Renier's discussion of what he called "accepted history" also follows the same pattern of thought; namely, that historians—sometimes with deliberate intent, but often in the normal course of pursuing their own research—check, corroborate, refute, or modify what other historians have done.[20] Renier emphasized that the historian must not regard "accepted history" as immutably valid, and quoted Dewey to the effect that the material must be adjusted to new discoveries and not the other way around. So long as this is done, every major historical occurrence and event will have a multiplicity of observers, using this word as Mandelbaum did rather than in the sense of eyewitness, and the margin of error will be reduced. The result will not be certainty, only a higher degree of probability because, as Father D'Arcy has warned, the degree of probability is the description of a mental attitude, not the attribute of the event.[21]

[19] G. M. Trevelyan, *The Present Position of History* (London: Longmans, 1927), p. 7.

[20] G. J. Renier, *History: Its Purpose and Method*, pp. 88 ff.

[21] M. C. D'Arcy, S.J., *The Meaning and Matter of History* (New York: Meridian Books, 1961), pp. 52, 53. Father D'Arcy later suggested (p. 56) that, "In reliving the past and interpreting it after judicial scrutiny of the evidence with a sympathetic understanding we graze truth."

These several arguments and conflicting opinions, stemming in large measure from the obvious fact that an historian cannot use the experimental method, all miss a more significant distinction between the historian and the scientist. The historian seeks to move from the present to the past; the scientist, from the present to the future. Although scientific experimentation may be used to verify past knowledge, its essence is the seeking of new knowledge: to discover what will happen, or if such and such will happen or can be made to happen under certain conditions. The scientists may, for example, hypothecate that certain changes can be produced in a substance by irradiation. They then set up an experiment, controlling insofar as possible all parameters, to test the hypothesis. It is also, of course, a frequent function of experimentation to attempt to isolate from general conditions those specifics which produced certain results. The purpose in both cases is forward looking.

The historian also wishes to advance knowledge, but he is by definition attempting to advance knowledge about what has been. He may desire this knowledge solely for its own sake, but he is more likely to feel that the past has a causal connection with the future; that what men believe has happened directly affects their anticipation of what may happen, and that this anticipation affects both actions and plans. An avowed purpose of American actions *vis à vis* the

Soviet Union in 1961 was to make impossible repetition of the type of misunderstandings which many historians insisted had led to war in the past. In this sense, the historian may also be looking forward as well as backward, but he has no techniques for altering the past or, if one may use a gardening term, "forcing" the future. Perhaps his limitations and his uncertainties may seem less damning now that physical scientists are finding fewer certainties as they probe their new frontiers of hot elements, strange particles, matter-anti-matter, and outer space.

The inability of the historian to derive laws, to predict with assurance that one phenomenon will follow upon another, to measure facts and to arrange them in causal sequences, and to supply unchallengeable solutions to problems has often been adduced as proof that history must be an art because it isn't a science. This assumes, of course, the ability of the physical scientist to accomplish all these facts. It is also, as Salvemini has pointed out, the equivalent of declaring that art is unsuccessful science. He added that the common assumptions that scientists know everything, have no doubts, experience no failures, are immune from reliance upon hypotheses, and are without biases are false. The more complex the material phenomena, said Salvemini, the less are scientists able to test them and to make certain forecasts. He concluded that doubtful spots are clearly more numerous in the study of human affairs, but that such spots also exist in the sciences.[22] Salvemini held with J. S. Mill that the "moral sciences"—Mill's phrase which Salvemini interpreted to include history and the social sciences—though inferior in exactness to the physical sciences, are truly sciences. Professor Morris Cohen took a similar position, but set different qualifications.

> If 'science' means knowledge based on the most careful examination of all the available evidence, the scientific historian certainly aims at such knowledge, and his work can be judged by the extent to which he attains his aim.[23]
>
> . . . the synthesis of the conscientious historian is like the synthesis of the scientist. . . . To the extent that historic investigation is controlled by the strictest rules of evidence, testing

[22] Gaetano Salvemini, *Historian and Scientist* (Cambridge: Harvard University Press, 1939), pp. 99 ff., 117 ff., 131 ff. Recent developments in physics and chemistry suggest that though the methodologies may be increasingly precise, the findings—at least in certain areas—are less certain. In other words, as physical sciences move forward into the unknown, scientists find themselves approaching a situation long familiar to historians.

The preceding paragraph, as well as those which follow immediately, owe much to Salvemini's book and to Professor Morris R. Cohen's, *Meaning of Human History*.

For a distinguished scientist's view on the subjectivity of many scientists, see: René Dubos, *The Dreams of Reason: Science and Utopias* (New York: Columbia University Press, 1961).

[23] Cohen, *op. cit.*, p. 36.

> every proposition by the extent to which it has been verified in observation or experiment, it may be properly called scientific.[24]

One suspects that those who disagree with Cohen might take the position that the key words in the quoted sentences are "if," "conscientious," and "to the extent." If science means the discovery of general laws, rather than knowledge based on carefully evaluated evidence, then history, which does not derive laws, is not a science. Specification of a conscientious historian presupposes that some are not conscientious, and therefore one can speak accurately only in particular cases: Historian X is conscientious, and may be called a scientist; Historian Y is not conscientious, and so is not a scientist. "To the extent," in like fashion, assumes a variation which requires particularization for accuracy. These objections are valid, but if applied literally they would reduce the whole matter to an *ad hominem* basis. This might, in some respects, be a good thing. If so, it ought also to be applied to those who profess the physical sciences. If Physicist A is conscientious, efficient, competent, he is a scientist; otherwise, he is not. Chemistry, in the hands of Chemist A is a science; in the hands of an inefficient, incompetent, unconscientious chemist, chemistry is not a science. This line of reasoning concentrates on

[24] Cohen, *op. cit.*, p. 32.

dissimilarities, which are undeniable, to the point of ignoring equally real similarities. This limits discussion to persons, and excludes the possibility of discussing the fields which the persons profess. Attractive as this may seem at first glance, reflection shows its impracticality.

Although Cohen spoke of historical investigation as being scientific in certain cases, he explicitly denied that history is a science like physics, or that the subject matter of history is laws or repeatable patterns of human behavior. Those who insist on this, he said, are confusing history with sociology. Although the historian's aim is not the establishment of law, he must assume the existence of causal and other laws. In this respect, history is an applied science like geology, medicine, or engineering except that the historian seldom states explicitly the laws which he assumes. One can no more eliminate laws from history than one can eliminate historical elements from science.[25] The scientist uses a special kind of history, the record of how

[25] Cohen, *op. cit.*, pp. 37, 38, 41. Essentially the same position was also taken by Professor Ernest Nagel who held that the natural sciences are not "exclusively nomothetic," and that history is not "a purely ideographic discipline." Nagel drew an analogy between history and theoretical science, on the one side, and medical diagnosis and physiology, or geology and physics, on the other side. Ernest Nagel, "Some Issues in the Logic of Historical Analysis," in Patrick Gardiner, *Theories of History*, pp. 374, 375.

other scientists have sought to solve a particular problem or set of problems. The mathematician uses concrete material as a springboard from which to jump into abstractions. The historian uses abstract material, including laws, in the definition, analysis, and verification of historic facts. His attempts to reconstruct these facts are subject to objective conditions; he does not create "facts" out of some inner experience. Historic facts do not change, "What has happened cannot 'unhappen,'" but the hypotheses about these facts may change. Facts do not explain themselves either to historians or to scientists. Ideas and hypotheses are essential not only in suggesting explanations, but also in suggesting what to look for and where to look.[26]

Neither the historian nor the scientist is a mere collector of facts; each must select on the basis of relevance, and each must seek to place the isolated fact in context. To begin with a selected fact or facts does not mean that either the historian or the scientist cannot function objectively nor give an adequate and valid account. In fact, if the inquiry were not selective, it would be pointless. The establishment of relevance, the placing in context, require a search for causality which means for the historian not a relation between an occurrence and some universal law, but the relation between occurrences or events. The historian cannot absolutely exclude the possibility of chance or of coin-

[26] Cohen, *op. cit.*, pp. 43, 48, 50, 67–69, 78.

cidence, but neither may he properly refuse to consider causality. The failure by the historian to achieve perfection, to attain certainty, to exclude all personal bias should neither discourage him from making the effort to find causal relationships nor be regarded as automatically invalidating all historical explanations. These limitations should keep him constantly alert and decently humble. Usually they do. "Better than most scholars, the historian knows that human motivation, like causation, is a complex and elusive process." The unlikeliness of arriving at definitive answers is all the more reason for carefully exploring and evaluating all possibilities.[27]

Lewis B. Namier once described history as ". . . 'the most difficult of all sciences,' because of its enormous range and the variety of phenomena it covers, and because of the inherent difficulties of its techniques." [28] The theme of the infinite complexity of history compared to an alleged straightforwardness of the physical sciences is recurrent. Cohen wrote of the "simple, repeatable patterns of physics or physical laws" which appear to have no counterpart in history.

[27] Cohen, *op. cit.*, pp. 96, 98, 102, 111; Nagel, *loc. cit.*, pp. 337, 378, 382. The quotation is from William L. Langer, "The Next Assignment," *AHR*, LXIII, 2 (January, 1958), pp. 283–304; p. 302.

[28] Lewis B. Namier, *Personalities and Powers* (New York: Macmillan, 1955), p. 9.

Professor Frederick Teggart, in one of his early works, stated the alleged distinction this way.

> Science sorts phenomena in order to identify processes. . . . it attacks the world piecemeal, and dissects and isolates strand after strand from the totality of things, on the assumption that the whole is like a cable—but what the cable is for, how it comes to be made up of fibers and strands, and between what points it stretches, are questions that Science regards as outside its province and beyond its ken.
>
> History narrates the specific acts of individuals, but always in relation to wider issues; the individual with whose acts it is concerned stands, if but for a moment, in a definite relation to the life and honor of the group of which he is a part.[29]

The same theme, but without the stated comparison with science, was put forward in a different context by Professor Butterfield.

> The genesis of historical events lies in human beings. The real birth of ideas takes place in human brains, the real reason why things happen is that human beings have vitality. [Peoples' thoughts, desires, and actions produce events.] Economic factors, financial situations, wars, po-

29 Teggart, *Prolegomena to History, loc. cit.*, pp. 166, 168, 176.

> litical crises do not cause anything, do not do anything, do not exist except as abstract terms and convenient pieces of shorthand. . . . It is men who make history—who really do things. All interpretations of history must be construed in the light of this fact.[30]

Over fifty years ago, the British historian, A. F. Pollard, drew a comparison which seems to include, at least *in posse*, the points made by both Teggart and Butterfield.

> History is not an exact science. Nothing that is real and concrete can be exact. Mathematics are exact, but only because they deal with abstractions. Two may be equal to two in arithmetic, but they are generally unequal in real life; no two men are exactly equal to two other men. . . . But truth that deals with concrete things is always relative; absolute truth is an abstract ideal not attained in practical human affairs, and therefore

[30] Herbert Butterfield, *History and Human Relations* (New York: Macmillan, 1952), pp. 66, 67. *Cf.* the statement by the French sociologist Maurice Halbwachs: "Each [individual] feels them [general controlling factors] because they are felt by the group he is a member of, and their shape and intensity are brought about by the conditions peculiar to the group and its structure and regulations [*sic;* relations?] with other groups." *The Psychology of Social Class*, Claire Delavenay, tr. (Glencoe: The Free Press, 1958), pp. 20, 21.

> not attainable in their history. History deals with an infinite number of variant facts, just as grammar does with an infinite number of variant uses; generalizations deduced from these facts, like grammatical rules deduced from these uses, are all incomplete, and partially false; there are exceptions to every rule.[31]

It would be unwise to presume that mathematicians or linguists would accept Pollard's characterizations of mathematics and grammar, or that physical scientists would either agree with Teggart, or would accept the general thesis that their disciplines were simpler. Even a superficial knowledge of modern physics and chemistry—not to mention such hybrids as astrophysics, geophysics, biophysics, and biochemistry—is enough to dispel impressions of their simplicity. There is, however, an observable aspect, which applies to scientists rather than to sciences, and which supports the thesis. When some physical scientists turn from their own fields and attempt to apply the criteria of their sciences to human affairs they often display an extreme naiveté and a complete lack of understanding about human motivations and actions. Some engineers, and other applied scientists, when

[31] Albert F. Pollard, *Factors in Modern History* (first edition, 1907; third edition, 1932; reprinted, Boston: Beacon Press, 1960), pp. 35, 36.

designing systems to be operated by men sometimes seem to take into account all except the human factor.[32]

Why should history be anything but history? Does anyone ask: Is science art? Is literature philosophy? Is chemistry language? Is biology medicine? Is physics history? All knowledge and learning are attempts to relate something to man, or man to something. They form an unending tapestry in which different scholars choose to trace different patterns, or to unravel different threads. There are necessarily many ways of or-

[32] For example, some physical scientists have been attracted to what they took without serious examination to be the "scientific precision of Communism." Others, making their first ventures into the field of international relations, have failed to recognize that human behaviors may be emotional in origin. This leads to the error of equating what man rationally "should" do with what he may choose to do. One must learn to look for both rational and emotional causes and behaviors in analyzing human actions.

An illustration of the second point is the design of an aerial reconnaissance system which depends on visual recognition to supply key information, but which places the observer in an aircraft so constructed that the requisite visual recognition is always difficult and uncertain and often impossible. The growing recognition of such blunders has led to the development of a special field under the horrendous label of "human engineering."

To pursue this one step further, there is an apocryphal army formula for determining the adequacy of special packaging for delicate equipment. "After all the scientific tests and calculations have been made, give the package to the nearest GI with orders to carry it for a day, using extreme care in handling. If the equipment survives, the packaging is adequate."

ganizing knowledge, none of which is complete in itself nor independent of all others. There is philosophy in literature, and the writings of some philosophers are literature. There is historical science, in the sense of systematic and purposeful review of past accomplishments in the sciences, including general reviews covering a whole field or fields as well as reviews which are limited to sub-fields or even to specific problems.[33] There is also scientific history in the sense that historians use methods of analysis and problems solving analagous to, or derived from the methods of science.

There are differences, of course, enjoined by the purposes of the study and by the subject material. An his-

[33] For example: Morris Kline, *Mathematics in Western Culture* (New York: Oxford University Press, 1953). According to its preface, this book was written, ". . . to advance the thesis that mathematics has been a major cultural force in Western civilization."; Richard S. Kirby *et alii, Engineering in History* (New York: McGraw-Hill, 1956). This is described by its publisher as a history of the interaction of human societies and the progress of engineering. Other examples include: F. Sherwood Taylor, *A History of Industrial Chemistry* (London: Heinemann, 1957); Friedrich Klemm, *A History of Western Technology*, tr. by D. W. Singer (New York: Charles Scribner's Sons, 1959); Abbott P. Usher, *A History of Mechanical Inventions*, rev. ed. (Cambridge: Harvard University Press, 1954); F. Sherwood Taylor, *An Illustrated History of Science* (London: Heinemann, 1955); J. F. Scott, *A History of Mathematics* (London: Taylor and Francis, 1958); and George A. Modelski, *Atomic Energy in the Communist Bloc* (Melbourne: Melbourne University Press, 1959). Only parts of the last book are historical.

torian, for instance, does not seek to establish the theoretical explanation for, nor the practical applications of tunnel diodes. He strives to produce "an orderly account of past events and of the people who participated in them, with a reasoned explanation of why things happened as they did." [34] This requires the historian, among other efforts, to define his problem; to collect data; critically to test and evaluate the data; to correlate the accepted data and to develop concepts or hypotheses based on them; to seek new data on the basis of the concepts and for the purpose of checking the concepts; and so on until he combines facts, probabilities, and explanations into a narrative. This is not essentially unlike the procedure of the

[34] The quotation is from T. S. Brocon, "Herodotus and His Profession," *AHR*, LIX, 4 (July, 1954), pp. 829–43; p. 830. Professor Mandelbaum has offered a different view of the proper subject matter of history, viz.: ". . . understanding and delineating the nature of specific societies and the changes which have taken place in these societies." Maurice Mandelbaum, "Concerning Recent Trends in the Theory of Historiography," *Journal of the History of Ideas*, vol. 16 (1955), pp. 506–17; p. 516. Mandelbaum takes the general position, which I share, that the actions of most individuals, as individuals, do not affect society in the large. The effects on society are produced when a number of individuals feel and act in like fashion. The number required to produce the effect varies with the circumstances, including the amount of fervor and the degree of unity and/or organization. A relatively few disciplined, devoted and affectively organized individuals can have a disproportionately great effect on a society (or group) which is at sixes and sevens.

scientist who is studying tunnel diodes. The historian used some methods which were akin to those of the scientist, and the latter began his study with what he called a "literature survey," by which he meant that he studied the history of past scientific experimentation on and theorizing about diodes. Broad similarities in methodology, however, do not necessarily produce equal precision or certainty in findings. The historian seeking to learn how and why L. Esaki of Japan discovered tunnel diodes will be less sure and less precise in his finding than the scientist who set out to study the diodes themselves.

A very large part of the difference in results stems not from an ability to derive or use universal laws, nor from a precision of methodology and techniques, nor from some qualities of personality and character which led one man to become an historian, the other a scientist. It arises from quantitative and qualitative differences in the information with which the two scholars work. "Universal laws" sometimes have a disconcerting way of turning out to be a good deal less than that. Methodologies and techniques may prove to have unexpected limitations or imperfections. Scientists, as well as historians, are subject to subjective influences —a point which will be reverted to shortly. But the historian is more likely than the scientist to be hampered by the amounts and kinds of available data.

The historian works with records [35] which he has not created, and does not control. An acid test of craftsmanship in historical research is the ability to uncover information in other than the obvious places, but there are limits to what ingenuity and imaginativeness in research can accomplish. Some occurrences and more frequently, some of the links between occurrences are never recorded, either because they seem too trivial, or by reason of chance. The records of other occurrences may be destroyed, forgotten, lost, mislaid, not physically available to the researcher, or not intelligible to him. The part played by chance in history is controversial, but few would dispute that chance has a major role in determining what is recorded and what records survive or are available. The historian cannot, by experimental or other methods, create new records. He must work with what he can find; he can literally know no better. If there is no record, or if the historian is ignorant of it or unable to use it, there will be a gap in his knowledge. Fortunately, there are multiple records for most events and many occurrences so that lack of one, while it may be in some degree crippling, is not necessarily fatal to the inquiry. In some instances, however, the missing records might be the keys to other

[35] I have used "records" as being more familiar to non-historians than "sources." Historians usually speak of "sources," reserving to "records" a more precise and technical meaning.

locks. No doors in history are secured with only a single lock, and no one key will open all the locks. If the gaps in the records are not too numerous nor too wide, the historian may seek to fill them by a sort of interpolation, but this always introduces the possibility of error.

Historians who deal with more recent periods, or with very large subjects sometimes face problems rising from a superabundance of records. The tasks of selection, which in itself involves critical evaluation; of later, more precise evaluation; of collation and correlation then become staggering. Is the potential error greater when one has to make very many judgments as in this case, or when a paucity of records compels one to make fewer but perhaps more significant guesses? The answer is uncertain. What is certain is that the necessity of making judgments—or estimates, or guesses, or interpretations—introduces into any scholarly effort, historical or scientific, the subjective element.

Each scholar in pursuit of his specialty, and every person in the course of his daily life, proceeds from within his own reality world. The individual's reality world is the psychological matrix from which his behavior stems, and which guides his purposeful actions. It is created by each for himself in the process of living, through transactions with the world around him. Its major ingredients are the assumptions, the aspirations, and the apprehensions which largely determine how a person will perceive a situation. The reality world is not static, though it may change so slowly and unevenly as to give that impression; it is fluid, subject to change in response to what the engineer would call feedbacks.

One of the significant functions performed by the reality world is to filter the stimuli, great and trivial, physical and abstract, which constantly assail us all. We learn in the process of our transactions which stimuli we must heed in order to accomplish certain purposes, which we may ignore temporarily or in part, and which we may ignore completely. Sometimes this means being aware of only a single stimulus; at other times, it means an awareness of many stimuli and their interrelations. The transaction of the moment determines which it is. This is commonplace, not esoteric. It is what we are talking about when we say that we have been sensitized to such and such an occurrence. The phenomenon called selective sleep, which has been experienced by most persons, is an excellent illustration. A mother may sleep through a thunderstorm, but be wakened by the whimper of her baby. A sailor may, in one situation, sleep through the blowing of a foghorn but waken when it stops; a contrary situation would reverse the selection. Humans literally have the capability of hearing what they wish to hear, seeing what they wish to notice, and grasping—within limits—what they wish to understand.

This selectivity operates in research, though modified by the results of special training, by conscious adherence to the canons of scholarship and by a deliberate effort to avoid or minimize bias. Every experienced researcher will recognize this operation, though he may not choose to express it the same way. It is what makes it possible to scan pages and books. It is why the eye fastens upon a word or phrase. It is what explains individual subjectivity, for each scholar has his own reality world.

Although each person creates for himself his private reality world, and although the uniqueness of this private world is never wholly lost, overlappings and similarities exist among the reality worlds of those who share a common background, or a common training, or common hopes and fears. If there were no such overlapping, communication among persons would fail. It is a truism, but only a partial truth, to say that no one can know what is in another's mind. If this were wholly true, human intercourse would necessarily cease. We can grasp enough of what another has in mind to carry on the business of everyday life, though we may not always understand enough to guarantee success. Our comprehension is always somewhat faulty and sometimes wholly so, but we have, by and large, learned to live within its limitations. This could not be unless there were some practical way of transactional communication, and such communication must rest on partially shared reality worlds.[36]

This partial sharing creates, in varying degrees, a group reality world. Those who partake in it will, within broad limits, make similar selection from stimuli affecting the group, operate on the basis of like assumptions, arrive at closely related perceptions, and act accordingly. This is the root of what might be called "group subjectivity," and explains partially why each generation feels called upon to write its own history. In this sense, and within these limits, Croce's view that historical events vibrate only in the present is correct. But there is more here than what Beard called "the frame of reference in the mind of the selector," which he thought "inexorably controlled" the historian. The group subjectivity produced by the group reality world never has perfect control because individual subjectivity, rooted in the personal reality world, always produces some variants. If it were literally true without any qualification that all scholarly interpretations were governed by the socio-economic and/or

[36] The immediate aim of questionnaires, inquiries, interrogations, and public opinion polls is to get inside the reality worlds of others for the purposes of communication; often with some other ultimate goal in view. See also the discussion of reality world in the next essay, pp. 134 ff.

political situation in which the scholar lived, only one interpretation would be offered by all in that situation. Moreover, the only limits on interpretation would be those set by the situation. Neither supposition accords with experience. Even Soviet scholars in the field of genetics arrived at different interpretations. The time came when they could no longer openly express their differences.[37] Subsequent events indicate that the differences may have been suppressed but not extirpated. The same series of happenings also showed the presence of another limitation upon interpretations: namely, that the interpretations must fit the facts, and that some do so better than others.

Historians are not scientists nor is history a science, but both disciplines are scholarly, and those who profess them are scholars. This is not to say, of course, that all scholars come equally close to the ideal, nor that all are equally effective. There have been, and there are, unscholarly historians and unscholarly scientists, but in the main, both share the same great goal—the search for truth. Both are subject to the limitations of their private and group reality worlds, which is another way of saying that each is in some measure

[37] "I, as a Party member, do not consider it possible for me to continue to hold views which have been declared erroneous by the Central Committee of our Party."—Anton Zhebrak. In the brief "thaw," the Lysenko-Michurin doctrines ceased to command the open adherence of all Soviet geneticists, a situation which shows some signs of being reversed once more.

subjective and that neither has a monopoly upon objective scholarship. Their general methods of approach and problem solving are more similar than is usually realized though they necessarily differ in specific techniques. One does not ask the same questions about the nature of nuclear fission and fusion as about the effects of these phenomena on the affairs of men. Different questions, different skills, different data are required, but the successful exploration of both problems demands the same qualities of curiosity, intellectual integrity, persistence, responsibility, and the capacity for conscientious hard work. Some of the confusion and argumentation over "is history a science?" has arisen from non-recognition of these commonalities; some, paradoxically, from non-recognition of differences; and some from misunderstandings of both. As to the misunderstandings and the non-recognition of dissimilarities, there is a possible analogy with sports. A man who had in mind only the scoring system of football or baseball would be bound to conclude that the golfer who scored a hundred had played far better than his opponent whose score was only seventy-five. The failures to recognize similarities, in addition to those already mentioned, also include the following.

It has been supposed by some that the historian's business is to find out "all that has happened." His inability to do so is used to support the charge that since he cannot know everything, he cannot really know anything. This is silly. An historian does not aspire to learn all about all of the past, but only about that part of the past on which his attention is focussed. Of course this involves selectivity and subjective judgment, just as it does when a scientist picks certain phenomena as the subject of his research. A like reply may be made to the charge that the historian "amputates reality" by selecting a time period or a limited subject scope and excluding all else. This is indeed an arbitrary action in the sense that the decisions have to be made by a person because they are not inherent in the material. It happens, as Professor Cohen observed, that "The seamless web of history may be ripped into disordered fragments by a clumsy historian," but he added, "or divided into significant parts that reveal definite patterns to eyes incapable of infinite vision." [38] Is there any reason for supposing that the same kinds of alternatives do not exist in science, and have not been chosen by scientists? The historian, as noted above, must sometimes attempt to interpolate or hypothecate to fill in the gaps in his facts. This must obviously be done with diffidence and great caution, not because history is so imprecise but because it is so varied that the area of possible error in hypothecation is wide.

The thorniest problem arises when the historian assumes the task, which he cannot properly avoid, of

[38] Cohen, *op. cit.*, p. 66.

appraisal and evaluation. He must, in making selections, judge the relevance, importance, and reliability of assorted data; in organizing his information, he must make judgments about relationships; and he must at least attempt to decide what alternatives there might have been, if any.[39] Such decisions involve precisely those value judgments which are so largely determined by the scholar's reality world. One must, however, have a standard in order to decide what is relevant, significant, and reliable.[40] The judgments do not inhere in

[39] This is a very tricky point, because history is the story of what happened, not of what might have happened. But, as Cohen has pointed out, ". . . all practical activity involves the weighing of alternatives only one of which is realized." "Causation and Its Application to History," *loc. cit.*, p. 20. In another place, he observed that, "We can understand the significance of what did happen only if we contrast it with what might have happened." *The Meaning of Human History*, p. 80.

One illustration involving this problem concerns the *zemstva* reform made by Tsar Alexander II. This was bitterly criticized on the ground that it favored the nobility, retained the predominance of the upper classes, and was unjust and ungenerous to the peasant majority. There was truth in the allegations, and subsequent Russian governments made the matter worse. But consider the situation at the time of the original reform (1864). Serf emancipation had destroyed the local "government-by-landlord," and some alternative had to be found. The newly emancipated peasants were in no position to assume the task. There was, in short, no viable alternative to continuing to assign most of this responsibility to the upper classes.

[40] This may have been what Professor Conyers Read had in mind when he wrote, ". . . [the] first requisite for an historian

the facts, but to be valid they must accord with the facts. Historians themselves are very sensitive, on the whole, to the intrusion of moral judgments in historiography. Professor Pollard wrote as follows on this point.

> There must be something radically wrong in historical methods and assumptions which lead honest men to diametrically opposite conclusions from the same body of evidence. And the fundamental misconception seems to be the idea that historical events are the expression of moral judgments.
>
> If we adopt that view, we shall always be driven to emphasize the success of a principle in which we believe, and to explain away the success of one in which we do not, lest our admissions should weaken our belief in the efficacy of our principles. Hence the constant explanation of the triumph of causes which we dislike by reference to tyranny and corruption exercised by the few over the many; because it is so much more comforting to believe that a few men were wicked than that the majority voluntarily embraced or acquiesced in what we think to be wrong. . . . While history

---

is a sound social philosophy." "The Social Responsibilities of the Historian," *AHR*, LV, 2 (January, 1950), pp. 275–85; p. 285.

> provides a sound basis of politics . . . its common employment as a basis of moral instruction is open to serious criticism.[41]

The concept of the reality world, and particularly of a group reality world, provides a sounder explanation than Pollard's of why other men voluntarily embrace, or acquiesce in, what we consider to be wrong. They assent to, or more actively identify themselves with what makes sense in terms of their assumptions, aspirations, and apprehensions. It is not necessary to endorse what they do, but neither is it necessary to judge their actions to be wicked.[42] What is involved here, aside from the use of the reality world concept in place of moral judgment, is a clearer view of the difference in meaning and in demands upon the scholar of neutrality and impartiality. To be neutral may mean nothing more than being neither the one thing nor the other; that is, indifferent. To be impartial means to be fair, just, equitable in discovering and displaying all the facts, those which run counter to one's preferences as well as those which support them. It is improper to demand that the historian be or pretend to be indifferent to tyranny, corruption, slavery, and similar behaviors. But it is highly proper to demand that he

[41] Albert F. Pollard, *Factors in Modern History*, pp. 9, 10.

[42] But *cf.* Professor C. V. Wedgwood's verdict that ". . . insistence upon a moral standard is necessary." *Op. cit.*, p. 54.

recognize that what seems in his reality world to be slavery may in another's reality world appear as security.

If being neutral means only that one does not indulge nor desire to indulge in judgments of good and evil, right and wrong, it is easier for a scientist than for an historian to be neutral. But it is hard to believe that the scientists at Almagordo were indifferent to the results of the first atomic explosion. The records, in fact, indicate that they were not. Insofar as a scientist cares which way an experiment goes, he cannot be said to be neutral. The alleged distinction that scientists are neutral about their work while historians are unneutral lacks validity. Impartiality is, in both cases, a very different matter. It seems appropriate to let Professor Cohen, to whom this essay already owes much, have a final word.

> The safeguard against bias in the writing of history, as in the natural sciences, is not to indulge in useless resolutions to be free of bias but rather to explore one's preconceptions, to make explicit, to consider their alternatives, and thus to multiply the number of hypotheses available for the apprehension of historical significance.[43]

[43] Cohen, *The Meaning of Human History,* p. 80.

IV

Recurrent Patterns in History

> Gravitation: any two material particles or bodies, if free to move, will be accelerated towards each other.
>
> $E = MC^2$: the Einstein equation for the interconversion of mass and energy.

THESE CLASSIC EXAMPLES illustrate feats of the physical scientists which cannot be matched by historians. The law of gravitation, as quoted above, is valid because it comprises the findings of a very large number of observations and experiments. It says, in effect: so far as is now known, all freely moving material particles and bodies behave in the manner stated; there have been no significant contrary observations, and none are currently anticipated. Historians cannot reach the same certainty of conclusions concerning past human affairs partly because historians cannot repeat an occurrence or an event under controlled conditions, but mostly because human affairs involve too many variables, contradictions, and unknowns.[1] Consider, as an example of the order of magnitude of variables and unknowns, a series of relatively simple occurrences which give an impression of recurrence if not of repetition: namely, scheduled air flights between two major cities.

The flights will show certain significant similarities. The cities do not move appreciably in relation to each other. All the flights are made by heavier-than-air, air-breathing aircraft, and we shall stipulate that the sample be limited to aircraft of the same design. We shall further stipulate, in order to reduce the number of variables, that each aircraft be adjudged airworthy by experts, that there is no significant overloading of any aircraft in the sample, that all crews are certified as professionally competent, and that the published schedules for all flights are comparable. Does it then follow that Flight 616 on the 29th is a recurrence or simple repetition of Flight 616 on the 19th, or of Flight 824 on either date? Every seasoned airline traveler

[1] *Occurrence* is used throughout this essay to indicate a happening of lesser scope and magnitude than an event. An *event* consists of many occurrences. The terms are entirely relative and imprecise. For example, a war may be called an event; a battle of that war, an occurrence. A battle, however, can also be considered to be an event made up of many occurrences. What constitutes an event to an individual is usually only an occurrence in terms of a larger unit.

knows that it does not. All kinds of things, large and small, can be different—runway conditions, visibility, weather-in-flight, air traffic, the behavior of crew and passengers, stresses and strains on the aircraft and the reactions of the structure and its components to these forces. It is possible to formulate laws of aerodynamics which permit prediction of the in-flight behavior of the aircraft, and laws of thermodynamics which permit prediction of the behavior of its power plant, but we do not know how to formulate laws which govern the flights as occurrences. The unknowns, the variables, the contradictions, the complexities are beyond us. The best we can do is to establish general probabilities on the basis of repeated incidents, and the margins of error are great.

Regular air flights as historical occurrences are simple when compared to such an historical event as a war. Those who have heard of both events are often tempted to compare Hitler's invasion of the Soviet Union in 1941 with Napoleon's invasion of Russia in 1812. In both cases, dual alliances, basically anti-British, were violated when one ally invaded the territory of the other. Neither attack was unexpected, but in neither case did the invaded nation make a strong initial defense despite advance warnings. Both Hitler and Napoleon had previously scored such military victories as to dominate the European continent west of the Russian/Soviet lands, but neither had been able to invade nor to defeat Great Britain. As a consequence of both events, persons who had no concern with high politics and no desire to be either conquerors or conquered suffered because of the acts of their rulers. The list of similarities can readily be extended to an impressive length, but the dissimilarities are equally impressive and significant.

There were three Great Powers—France, Russia, and Great Britain, and two almost Great Powers—Austria and Prussia, in 1812. By 1941, the last two were parts of Germany, which had also conquered and partially occupied France; and two new Great Powers overseas, the United States and Japan, took active parts in the second event. Stalin's absolute power at home was much greater than that of Tsar Alexander I, and the Soviet dictator also had faithful, disciplined followers around the world. The second invasion lasted longer, penetrated more widely and more deeply, involved far more persons and much more material, and contrasted in many other ways with the first. Since the personnel involved in 1941 obviously had to be different from that of 1812, to cite only one of the possible items, the second invasion could not have been a recurrence of the first. Other dissimilarities preclude calling the event of 1941 a repetition of that of 1812. Despite the similarities, each event was unique though certain similitudes and constants are discoverable. These are not, however, of the type to support the formulation of laws in the scientific or philosophical senses of that term.

As to the derivation of equations for the expression of universals like $E = MC^2$, other, but equally insurmountable, obstacles confront the historian as can be readily shown. One of the major problems in historiography is the absolute and relative evaluation and verification of reports, records, and—to use the historians' term—other sources. It would be very useful to have a formula for equating reliability.[2] The first steps are easy because they are completely arbitrary and abstract. Let W = one observer (witness or participant), 2W = two observers, etc.; and let R = one report (record or other source), 2R = two reports, etc.; and let R/W = one report by one observer, 4R/W = four reports by one observer, 4R/4W = four reports by four observers, etc. Now try to set up

[2] A previously quoted comment by Professor Mandelbaum is relevant here. "Historical events are therefore observed, and not only are they observed they are in many instances also recorded, by many men in many countries, and this is analagous to the repetition to which the events in the natural sciences are subjected. [Common observation and reporting add up to] . . . verification by repetition." Maurice Mandelbaum, *The Problem of Historical Knowledge: An Answer to Relativism* (New York: Liveright Publishing Corporation, 1938), p. 188.

The reader will gather from what follows that I think this analogy to be shaky, although multiple, independent reports which can be compared and cross-checked are among the most valuable sources an historian can have.

a meaningful equation. Are four reports by four observers four times as valid as one report by one observer? If so, the equation would read: $4R/4W = 4(R/W)$. What about $8R/4W$? Does this equal $2R/W$? If so, eight reports by four observers have the same value as two reports by one observer. This is obviously absurd unless one can assume equality among all observers and all reports, and such equality rarely exists in real life. In fact, it exists so rarely as to make the suggested equations nonsense.

Suppose, to carry this a step farther, we devise a system which rates the competence and reliability of observers on the basis of our knowledge of them on a scale running from A (most competent and most reliable) to E (least competent and least reliable). Reports are rated on a matching scale from 5 (most probable or plausible) to 1 (least probable or plausible). An A-5 rating is therefore the best; an E-1 the weakest. Does $5(E\text{-}1) = (A\text{-}5)$? That is, are five improbable or implausible reports by five incompetent or unreliable observers equal to one probable or plausible report by a competent, reliable observer? Unless it is assumed that the one never makes a mistake, and that the five are aways totally wrong, the answer isn't as simple as it may at first appear. The five reports may have been rated implausible because they dealt with something new which the highest rated observer may have missed or misunderstood. There are other possible variations. The point is that so many variables limit the validity of the rating scales, and invalidate the suggested equations.

If these observations are correct, or are accepted temporarily as the basis for continuing discussion, it follows that it is unrealistic to expect historians to formulate laws of history, or to derive universals, whether expressed in equations or by other means. Yet there are observable patterns of human conduct and of human activities, the stuffs of which history is made. It is difficult to find a satisfactory label for them. They are not *laws* in the sense in which philosophers and scientists speak of laws, nor in the sense in which the behavioral scientists seek universals which will support predictions. It is pretentious and too formidable to speak of them as *postulates;* and too vague to call them *variables.* They are more than *surmises,* as that word is generally used; but less than *deductions,* in the technical sense. *Inference* perhaps comes closer to being accurate, but does not fit precisely. *Patterns* may mislead by implying something obvious like the design appearing in a fabric. The recurrent patterns of history are not self-evident to the casual observer, although they may seem so when called to his attention. It is part of the historian's task to discern these patterns, if he can; to formulate them into hypotheses for repeated testing; and to present his findings—implicitly in his historical writing, or explicitly as in this essay—for the consideration by others.[3]

It has been said that an historian can only predict the past, and cannot do that with precision. There is one prediction, however, which an historian can make with confidence: namely, that two distinct but interrelated patterns will continue to appear in human affairs and, therefore, in history. They have been present from the beginning and will persist as long as life endures. They are abstractly disparate and mutually exclusive, but they are concretely linked. One is the pattern of change; the other, the pattern of continuity. It is impossible to discuss them simultaneously, but it is also impossible to keep them separate for long because one is a function of the other. Unless one can assume with tranquility that past and present are literal chaos consisting of simultaneous and consecutive, wholly fortuitous happenings, it is necessary to seek for and to recognize persistence. Whatever persists has continuity in some aspects; change in others.

[3] I have in mind something akin to a sentence once spoken in another connection by G. M. Trevelyan: "History is the open Bible: we historians are not priests to expound it infallibly: our function is to teach people to read it and to reflect upon it for themselves." *The Present Position of History* (London: Longmans, 1927), p. 5.

Strike a wooden match, watch it burn briefly, blow it out. The changes are obvious. It can no longer fulfill its original function, though it can be rekindled in another way. It is a burned match, to be sure, but it is still a match; it has not became a hoe handle. If the products of the burning have been carefully conserved, weighed, and the weight compared with the original, the two—as every schoolboy used to know—would have been found to be identical. The alternative to the concept of continuity plus change is the concept of repetitive juxtapositions of novel entities. Either you are the same person you were a year ago, plus or minus various qualities, or you have been 365 different persons or more—"new every morning, fresh every evening." This may sometimes seem an intriguing prospect, but it would soon create enormous practical difficulties.

Thinking in terms of human mortality, we talk of some things as unchanging—the everlasting hills and the eternal rocks, for example. Yet we know, even if we are not geologists, that hills erode, rocks crumble, and the face of the earth alters in appearance. Glaciers recede, coast lines rise and subside, and rivers shift their courses. Such changes are usually so slow as to go almost unremarked, but they can be measured. At the other extreme of speed are changes wrought by explosive forces in the twinkling of an eye. Geneticists seeking rapidity of change along with continuity, often work with fruit flies whose successive generations appear at very brief intervals. Human changes, in terms of speed, lie on the scale between the glaciers and the fruit flies but considerably closer to the latter. All men, and all groups and institutions which men create or organize, are constantly in flux. So, also, are all those objects designated as living. So is energy unless it is "at rest," and rest in this usage is imprecise and relative. *Being* is a process of *becoming*, that is, of change. History, which is the story of men, is therefore partly the story of changes and their concomitants. Some of the concomitants are uneven stresses and strains.

Institutions and organizations usually change more slowly than individuals, but changes in both are irregular in scope, speed, and nature. Changes are multiple, and are not always consistent with each other nor with an overall purpose. The multiplicity and inconsistency are responsible for some of the stress and strain, but human resistance to change is a more important cause. Professor Morris Cohen once described this resistance as inertia, and went so far as to state that, "Inertia is the first law of history, as it is of physics." [4] This is vivid, but inaccurate both as a "law

[4] Morris R. Cohen, *The Meaning of Human History* (LaSalle, Illinois: Open Court Publishing, 1947), p. 107. Also, "The dominant fact is that though people generally complain against the existing situation, inertia makes them unwilling to revolt or take other active measures to change the situation," pp. 63, 64.

of history," and because it implies passivity or purposelessness. Resistance to change is more often active and purposeful, although the purpose is not necessarily identified nor expressed by the resister. One of the purposes is the desire for security. The known, the routine, the familiar give a feeling of security which is often illusory but which is nonetheless real and comforting to the persons involved. We learn to place ourselves in the familiar situation. We know, as we say, where we stand. We do not know where we will stand in a changed situation, and this uncertainty induces a more or less temporary apprehension and sense of insecurity. If we have a choice, we will resist the change unless we have some assurance that it will at least leave us as well off as before. Even when the prospects are promising, we are likely to suffer short bouts of anxiety. There are individual variations in this as there are in most human behaviors. The range is from those who resist all change, however minor—who drag their feet and look longingly backward—to those who welcome change in the spirit of adventure. Security to the latter is presumably less important than the excitement of challenge. The majority, however, cling to the old and accept the new slowly and with at least passing regret.

One illustration of the comfort derived from the known will be familiar to everyone who has read and re-read, or told and retold stories to children. Attempts to paraphrase, or to shorten the story meet with immediate protests. The omission of a sentence, sometimes of a word, is greeted with displeasure. The child's sense of security is reinforced by repetition of the familiar; diminished by alteration of it. An example on a larger scale was the widespread and often violent resistance to the reforms in liturgy and ritual introduced into the Russian Orthodox Church by the Patriarch Nikon. Sections of both liturgies and ritual had become corrupted over the centuries, sometimes to the point of making no sense at all. To the Russian masses who regarded liturgies and rituals more as magic incantations than as divine worship, an alteration in the familiar formulae seemed a threat to the efficacy of the magic and therefore to the security of the people. There were other causes of the schism which the Nikonian reforms triggered in the Russian Church, but this subtle, pervasive resistance to change was one of the most important.

A second purpose served by resisting change is the conservation of human energy. It usually requires more energy to undertake the new than to continue with the old, and human energies are limited. If most of a person's strength is required to keep himself fed and sheltered, he will have little energy left for new ventures. This affects, also, the rate, the extent, and the unevenness of change. It may be necessary to change slowly, or by stages simply because there is not enough strength to accomplish it all at once. Similarly, it may be necessary to continue most routines in order to have enough energy to break away from one routine. This has been abundantly exemplified by the deliberate choice of the Communist rulers of the USSR to build up new, heavy industry while retaining the old ways in other activities. The resulting physical contrasts have frequently been remarked, but the internal stresses and strains are less easy to see. The coexistence of continuity and change in personal and institutional lives is productive of serious strains and grave problems.[5]

The resistance to change or, in some instances, the unfeasibility of change, the multiplicity and irregularity of change, and the necessity for using what is on hand, so to speak, all combine to produce the fact, as distinct from the concept, of continuity. Neither men, nor nations, nor lesser groups start with completely

[5] This situation is being repeated in all the "underdeveloped areas" which are seeking to make the quantum jump into "modernity." Not all have made the same choices as the Soviet Communist Party made for its subjects, but all are experiencing comparable stresses and problems.

Ignorance, slowness of comprehension—or the lack of it, and the absence of any clear purpose are all causes of resistance to change. It also happens that persons and institutions do not attempt changes simply because they can see no real alternative to what they have. They may in such cases desire change, but be unable to achieve it. The consequent frustration subjects the person or institution to strain, but will not produce action unless there is reasonable hope for improvement. Revolutions are not made by those who despair, but by those who hope.

clean slates. ". . . the past is on top of us and with us all the time . . . ," is the way Namier once phrased it. Cohen put it more formally: " . . . there are elements of identity between the present and the past. . . . The past literally continues into the present. Past conditions, such as old ideas and habits . . . continue to operate."[6] The continuity may be deliberate and purposeful, unintended or accidental, or inescapable under the given circumstances. It may also be pretended or exaggerated.[7] Purposeful continuities are

[6] Lewis B. Namier, *Avenues of History* (New York: Macmillan, n.d.), p. 2; Morris R. Cohen, *op. cit.*, pp. 63, 107.

[7] Namier made the sweeping generalization that, "While ideas outlive reality, names and words outlast both. . . . there are permanent elements in the lives of communities. . . ." *Op. cit.*, p. 3. His use of "permanent," as has been pointed out earlier, is imprecise. Permanence in human affairs is relative, not absolute.

The pretence or exaggeration of continuity can be illustrated by reference to the previous discussion of the Hitlerian and Napoleonic invasions of what is now the USSR. The Soviet regime publicized real and alleged similarities between the two as part of the propaganda effort to sustain and to enhance the morale of their subjects. The latter event was labeled, "The Second Great Fatherland War," and Soviet citizens were encouraged to emulate real or mythical feats of their predecessors. The Soviet historian, Tarlé, was forced to recant his considered and scholarly opinion that the war against Napoleon had not been a peoples' war and to declare the contrary. Other examples are the fabrications and exaggerations concerning Stalin's closeness to Lenin. The post-Stalin regime first attempted to dissociate itself from Stalin by denying continuity, but has now partially reversed itself and claims continuity in some lines.

readily seen in the retention of religious and secular rituals as well as in lesser, personal actions like "always" going to Grandma's for Christmas. Unintended continuities may arise from failures to carry out planned actions in full, or because the continuation is irrelevant to the immediate objective and is therefore ignored. The inability to execute actions as planned often stems from a failure to recognize human resistance to changes and the consequent persistence of habitual behaviors and beliefs. It is upon this rock that the efforts of reformers so frequently founder,[8] and even professional revolutionaries find it impossible to accomplish all the changes at once. No revolution —political, commercial, industrial, or scientific—ever makes a clean sweep of the old, nor do revolutionary changes affect all persons or institutions uniformly. There is a surprising amount of continuity in the midst of the greatest changes. One useful way of looking at this is embodied in the norm and value concept of history.

Social norms are both concrete and tangible, and abstract and intangible. The former include ways of making a living, media of exchange, food, clothing,

[8] It has often been suggested that one of the historian's proper services to his fellows is to bear witness to the fact of continuity and so to warn against unrealism and undue hopes. See, for example: Albert F. Pollard, *Factors in Modern History* (Boston: Beacon Press, 1960), p. 2.

shelters, means of transportation—in short, all the material paraphernalia of life in the particular group. Intangible norms include habits of thought and behavior, taboos, customs, and general attitudes, or responses to stimuli. Every group has, in the process of being, developed social norms which are accepted by the majority in the group, usually without question or thought of nonconformity.[9] Every person who joins the group, whether by birth or by immigration, must learn the norms of the group, and is expected to conform to them. Most persons do both. Some norms are imposed by terrain, soil fertility, climate, and other geographical situations. Wheat farming, brick dwellings, and silk clothing are obviously not the social norms of the Eskimos. Norms such as apprehensive-

[9] In the strictest sense, "group" could be held to mean any congeries of persons. It is not so used here. Small groups which affect only a few persons, and transitory groupings which do not endure long enough to affect the general behaviors of their members are both excluded. Exact figures cannot be set, but "group" is here used in reference at least to hundreds and more often to thousands of persons whose association is sufficiently formal and stable to last at least decades and usually generations. The word is not employed as a synonym for nation, first because a nation may include a number of groups, and second because social norms do not all stop at political boundaries. One finds, for example, many social norms which are identical in the United States and Canada. On the other hand, there are some significantly different social norms as between—again, for example—the Northeastern and the Southwestern states.

ness or hostility to neighbors are functions of proximity, or relative power, or past experiences. The general Norwegian antipathy to the rearming of the West Germans and the admission of the German Federal Republic to NATO arose mainly from recollections of the German occupation of Norway in World War II.

Each group, in addition to developing its own social norms, has also made certain judgments, or placed certain values upon these norms. Some ways of earning a living, for instance, are regarded as being more desirable than other ways. Certain occupations may carry taboos. An Indian professor does not expect to engage in any form of manual labor. To do so in a group in which labor is cheap, plentiful, and desperately in need of employment would bring disapproval from the group. Groups which think of themselves as "practical" and "dynamic," but which may be regarded by others as being "unduly materialistic," set high values on equipments and gadgets. Few Americans believe it improper or undesirable behavior to wish to acquire a new electrical appliance for the home, or a new car. The possession and use of such goods constitute an American social norm upon which American groups have placed a positive or favorable value. This may be contrasted with the findings of a recent study of Indian villagers, seventy per cent of whom thought that "electrical and mechanical conveniences will upset the happy life we Indians have always led." Eighty per cent of them said that "having more things simply adds to the unhappiness of the individuals"; ninety-three per cent that "life is better when the individual does not desire new things or more things." These Indian villagers, in other words, denigrated the social norms which Americans value highly.

Social norms and values are not static. As long as they have any vitality, they are in the process of change. Circumstances and the minority of nonconformists give rise to new norms and values which constantly challenge the old. Men find new ways of making a living; some are benefited and others are hurt by the change. Gas and oil gradually displace coal as fuel, and internal combustion engines take the place of steam engines. Clothing made from synthetic fibers breaks the monopoly of clothing made from natural fibers. Flour for home baking is no longer purchased by the barrel, but by small packages. The school-leaving age is raised, and higher education comes to be regarded as properly the right of the many rather than the privilege of the few. The development of the wheel shifts the burdens of porterage and permits a ready transfer of power. Serf emancipation in old Russia alters the legal status of millions from chattel property to free men, and puts in train a series of changes which are not completed a century later.

The changes are usually slow, imperfect, and incomplete. A few old norms and values are replaced by the new, but more often there is a partial modification rather than a replacement. Family ties are, for example, generally weaker in most groups now than they were fifty or a hundred years ago, but the old proverb about the relative thickness of blood and water still holds good. There are pockets of resistance in which the old norms and values persist longer than elsewhere. By and large, however, the majority within the group accustom themselves to the new and accept it, a process often made easier because the gradualness of the change conceals its extensiveness. There are exceptions all along the line, but there is sufficient conformity within the group to the norms and values of the group to validate limited generalizations about the group. Such generalizations do not deny the existence of exceptions nor the importance of the individual. It is action by individuals which, sometimes intentionally but more often unwittingly, initiates the challenges and brings the changes in the group's norms and values.

History may be thought of as the systematic study of the past social norms and values of a group or groups. The historian seeks to learn what the norms and values were at a given time or within a given period, to uncover their origins, and to trace the changes. He looks for ". . . clues that lead from known facts to antecedent and consequent conditions and thus enable him to push forward the frontiers of knowledge." [10] The

[10] The quotation is from Cohen, *op. cit.*, p. 38.

norm and value concept of history not only takes account of, but also makes use of the interrelated patterns of change and continuity. Isolated facts have meaning only within a larger framework which this concept provides. It is concerned with what was, not with what should have been, but it permits consideration of what alternatives, if any, may have seemed to exist. The concept is not tied to any particular schema, nor to any theory of cycles or progress, nor to any special set of moral judgments. It does, however, assume—contrary to Beard's thesis—that history is not chaos but a matter of discoverable patterns. The first two of these patterns are the dichotomous change/continuity which bears comparison with the "life/half-life" of the hot elements.

The third recurrent pattern—though the numbering is for convenience only and not in terms of occurrence or absolute importance—is the brotherhood of men. This is a tricky and highly variable pattern, often difficult to discern, and impossible to discuss with assurance. Physiologists and psychologists, as well as poets and prophets, attest to it; empirical evidence of the ability of utter strangers to communicate with each other, however imperfectly, provides an added confirmation. The difficulty arises partly from the implicit moral imperative of "brotherhood," which makes it simultaneously an expression of fact and an exposition of an ideal behavior, and partly from the further implications of interdependence and potentially correlative actions.[11]

Among the complications raised by the latter point is the quasi-physical, quasi-metaphysical problem of the effect on one action of another action which is unknown to those involved in the first. If I act in ignorance of A, whatever A may be, does A exist for me? The answer is both *no* and *yes*; *no*, in the sense that I cannot take A into account in planning, preparing, or executing my action; *yes*, in the sense that the existence of A, even though it is external to my consciousness, may vitally affect what I try to do. Suppose, for example, that I submit to a publisher an unsolicited manuscript which is of publishable quality. Suppose further that this publisher already has accepted a manuscript on the same subject and that this fact causes him to reject my manuscript. If he offers no explanation, I remain ignorant of the other manuscript. It continues to exist outside my ken, but it has frustrated my action.

Turning from this small matter to larger ones, have

[11] Professor Frederick J. Teggart developed an elaborate theory of correlations between events physically far removed from each other. It was his thesis that every outbreak on the European border of the Roman Empire was preceded by outbreaks either along the eastern borders or in western China. He argued the existence of a causal connection. See F. J. Teggart, "Causation in Historical Events," *Journal of History of Ideas*, III (1942), pp. 3–11; and *cf*. Morris R. Cohen, "Causation and Its Application to History," *loc. cit.*, pp. 12–29.

events in the recent history of the Far East—events of which the West was ignorant or of which it had only a very imperfect appreciation—affected the history of the West? The answer is again both *yes* and *no*; *no*, in the sense that the unknown Far Eastern events could not affect judgments, decisions, and actions planned; *yes*, if the events facilitated or frustrated actions initiated by the West during its period of ignorance. Western ignorance or misunderstanding of the nature, strength and intentions of the Chinese Communists meant that the West in general failed to assess correctly the developments taking place in China during the middle 1940's—developments which clearly affected western plans and actions. Two centuries earlier, the fall of the empire of the Great Mogul —also unknown or imperfectly known to the West of that time—significantly affected western history by opening India to western exploitation.

Slowly but steadily the evidence mounts that more men are increasingly aware of the realism in John Donne's famous words, "No man is an islande . . . but a part of the maine. . . ." The relevance of the point to this discussion is that the recurrent pattern of the brotherhood of men should constantly remind the historian that occurrences and events do not take place in a vacuum. It is not necessary to carry the search for interrelationships to absurd lengths, nor to attempt to correlate the ascension of a new Dalai Lama with the domestic histories of western nations. It is, however, salutary to recall now and then that the change in European fashions which sent beaver hats out of style affected the lives of both Indians and whites in North America. "And what should they know of England/Who only England know?"

It is possible to seek too far afield, and to assert too much in terms of the brotherhood of men. The connotation of brotherhood stresses resemblances and similarities sometimes to the point of ignoring what all have observed: that blood brothers are frequently unlike in appearance, character, and behavior. To speak of a recurrent pattern of brotherhood is not to insist that men are all alike nor that they are alike in all ways. It takes account of diversities as well as of commonalities. It suggests why and how historians, and others, look at the facts of human affairs from the inside, that is, by analogy with their own experiences. This can be extraordinarily misleading if one assumes that brotherhood of men means uniformity. The final significance to the historian of the recurrent pattern of brotherhood is, to paraphrase what Vico wrote over two centuries ago, that men ought to be able to understand history because history is made by men.

The fourth recurrent pattern is that men live by a multiplicity of faiths or accepted assumptions which range from the relatively simple and common to the more complicated and personal. Dictionaries define *faith* primarily in religious terms, and list it as a synonym for *belief* with the added note that *faith* implies a greater degree of certainty than does *belief*. To use *faith* as the equivalent of *accepted assumptions* is mildly unconventional and may be displeasing to the purist, but it offers a convenient ellipsis in place of a cumbersome explanation. The explanation, however, must be attempted because an understanding of this particular usage is vital to the discussion which follows.

Assumptions are the working tools by which men order their worlds and so make life possible. We assume, for example, that the sun will rise each morning and will set each evening. We have learned much about how and why these phenomena occur, and we have learned accurately to predict their daily time variations. We have accommodated our thinking to include the "white nights" and the "black days" of the polar seasons, that is, we recognize great variations in the lengths of days and nights; but we assume the continuing alternation of day and night. This alternation has taken place as far back as man's mind can run. Its continuation is a necessary condition to the only life we know, and the assumption that the alternation will continue in its orderly pattern is vital to sanity. This is an accepted assumption, relatively simple and virtually universal. We have faith, in the sense of a certain belief, that our assumption is correct and reliable.

Moreover, it is an assumption which we rarely recognize as such; which we take for granted, that is, as given by God, or by the nature of the universe, or by the conditions of life; and we almost never wonder about it.

The worn witticism, "Do you think it will rain? I dunno, it always has," expresses another general and common faith or accepted assumption, but one which includes a fractional element of doubt. Men have learned from tragic experiences that although it may always rain eventually, the rainfall may be too late or too scanty to serve men's needs. The earth bears evidences of climatic changes which forced men to remove themselves from certain areas. Many accepted assumptions seem so elementary, so basic, so obvious that we lump them all together, if we think of them at all, under the label, "facts of life." Genuine proverbs and folksayings are the distillations of accumulated human wisdom and experience. They are also statements of assumptions generally accepted by a group, and are parts of that group's norms and values.

There are also many more restricted assumptions which men habitually make and use: that of two objects seen together, the larger or the brighter is closer to the observer; that weight varies directly with size, and that the larger of the two objects is also the heavier of the two. Each of us has been accumulating such assumptions since babyhood as part of the process of living. Some are taught us in formal fashion; others we learn informally from repeated observations and experiences.

The distinguished social psychologist, Hadley Cantril, once defined assumptions as the "weighted averages of the registered effects of previous transactions." He amplified this in the following passage.

> The net result of our previous transactions is that we construct for ourselves an organized and interrelated pattern of assumptions which give continuity and significance to perceiving and serve as guides and bases for future behaving. Each specific transaction of living involves the participation of and reflects the presence of certain patterns of assumptions.
>
> We build up assumptions about things or objects, about individuals and groups, about institutions and ideologies, about nations and organizations, about cause-and-effect relationships, about the value-qualities of experience we believe will follow certain actions, and so forth. It should not be inferred that the individual is always aware of the participation of assumptions as functional variables in his perceiving and behaving. . . . Many of our assumptions are "subconscious." We may accept the world as we experience it as inherently given, without any recognition on our

> part that it is influenced by our unique past history. We may become aware of some of our assumptions only if we experience repeated disillusionment, frustrations, surprises, and disappointments as we strive to achieve our purposes.[12]

Several points may be further emphasized. Not only does the "organized and interrelated pattern of assumptions," which each of us develops, provide continuity and the basis for future actions, it is also indispensable to normal living. What indescribable confusion, frustration, and inefficiency would result if men could not use assumptions and so had to figure out each situation afresh and in detail. Sheer practicality is a

[12] Hadley Cantril and Charles H. Bumstead, *Reflections on the Human Venture* (New York: New York University Press, 1960), pp. 105–106.

I have long borrowed very freely from the work of Dr. Cantril and his associates and professional colleagues. Specifically, I owe to them the concepts of norms and values, assumptions, perceptions, and reality worlds. The debt has been so long accumulating, and over the years I have so completely adopted and adapted some of their ideas that I can no longer identify them all nor disentangle theirs from my own. My first introduction to the work of these scholars was a brief study by Muzafer Sherif, *The Psychology of Social Norms* (New York: Harper, 1936). During the ensuing quarter century I have experimented with applying this, and subsequently the other concepts to the study and teaching of history. In the process I have made my own not only some of their ideas, but probably some of their *ipsissima verba* as well.

sufficient reason why men live by a pattern of accepted assumptions or multiple faiths. The element of feedback is also significant both as a partial explanation of change, and as a partial explanation of causation in history. An event, or occurrence, or action which succeeds, or seems to, confirms the assumption, or assumptions, which underlay it. Every Soviet success in space, for instance, thus seems to Khrushchev, and millions of others, to prove the correctness of his assumption that the Soviet system is superior to all others. His reasoning presumably runs about as follows. Communism, because it is scientifically based, permits the most efficient possible use of national resources, including men. It is therefore superior to any other system. This is proved by the fact that the first man to orbit the earth was a product and symbol of the Soviet Communist system. The obverse is that repeated failures may lead to a re-examination and modification of the assumptions which guided the action. The human reluctance to change, discussed above, may explain why it usually takes many disappointments to produce a change in assumptions.[13]

[13] Determinists would presumably argue that external forces prevent those doomed to failure from changing their assumptions. Since I do not propose to enter the discussion of determinism *vs.* free will, I will simply state that one of my assumptions is that men cannot shift responsibility for their actions to some external force. I do not assume that men are free to make *any* assumptions they choose, nor to follow *any* course of action

The discussion of the fourth recurrent pattern has been in terms of individuals. This raises the problem of the role of the individual in history. At one extreme is the hero-in-history school, traditionally exemplified by reference to Carlyle, Froude, and, sometimes, Emerson.[14] At the other extreme are the absolute historical materialists, usually illustrated by reference to Marx.[15] Those named are not the only protagonists and practitioners of their respective views. Each has had many disciples and many opponents, and a whole range of positions fills the scale between these extremes. Engels himself backed away from absolute historical materialism when he admitted that "ideological spheres" may react upon the material forces which, in his view, produced them. The famous Marxist theoretician and early Bolshevik, Georgi Plekhanov, took the position that "great men" were the products of socio-economic forces but that they nonetheless played major roles in

---

which they may fancy. I assume the existence of limits though I cannot define them except in very general terms. A man may be too poor, for example, to move to an area of greater opportunity, or too unskilled to find a better job, and his poverty and ignorance may result partly from accidents or incidents which he could neither control nor avoid. But I also assume that within variable limits an individual may exercise some choice of behaviors.

14 "There is no History, only Biography."

15 "The history of all hitherto existing society is the history of the class struggle."

history. The *History of the Communist Party of the Soviet Union*, that *vademecum* of all the faithful, stresses the debt of the Bolshevik Revolution to Lenin. A recent article in the Soviet journal, *Problems of History*, declared that: "According to the teaching of Marxism-Leninism, people make history because they make their own life. . . ." [16] The other extreme view has also been modified, but the controversy continues over "Do men make events, or do events make men?" It will not be resolved by what follows.

Starting with the simple assumption that history is the story of people, one moves immediately into a complexity so vast as to be overwhelming. In the first place, there have been so many people that no one mind could ever encompass all their stories. Secondly, the actions and thoughts of most individuals are never recorded so that recovery of the individual stories would be impossible. Moreover, the actions of most individuals, as individuals, have a very limited range of effectiveness. Yet if history is the story of people, it must be the story of all people and not just of the favored, the famous, or the notorious. How does one

[16] F. D. Kretov, "The Question of Creating a Multivolume History of the USSR," *Voprosy istorii* (*Problems of History*), no. 2 (February, 1961), pp. 54–66. A condensed version, in English translation, appeared in vol. XIII, no. 13 (April 26, 1961), of *The Current Digest of the Soviet Press*, pp. 3–7. See also Robert V. Daniels, "Soviet Power and Marxist Determinism," *Problems of Communism*, IX, 3, pp. 12-18.

escape the paradox of believing in the worth and dignity of the individual and at the same time recognize the impossibility, not to mention the undesirability, of thinking of history only as billions of biographies?

The escape begins with a clarification of purpose and a recognition of limits inherent in the materials and in the ability to comprehend these materials. It has recently become fashionable to assemble a history of an occurrence or an event by interviewing as many of the participants as possible, or, when time has made interviews impossible, by reading diaries and letters. Bits and pieces culled from these sources are then synthesized, in accordance with an over-all plan of the author, into a narrative. If this is skilfully and scrupulously done, the result can be very entertaining and somewhat enlightening, and is certainly a form of historiography. If skill or integrity are lacking, the product is a mass of trivia or a morass of personalized mythologies. The method at best is of limited applicability and value. Even the most diligent can interview only a certain number of surviving participants so that the event must be one which is restricted in scope and duration. Dependence upon letters, diaries, and other personal records means dependence upon three kinds of chances: who chanced to make the records, what records happened to survive, and which of these the researcher was diligent enough and lucky enough to find and be able to use. The method is primarily that of the biographer, rather than of the historian who usually deals with a less circumscribed subject.

The subject matter of history is usually the actions of organized groups over a period of years, and the historian's usual purpose is to describe, analyze, and interpret what happened in and to the group within the specified time span. He is interested in individuals only insofar as their thoughts and deeds affected the group. The number of individuals who affect significant portions of the group decreases as the group increases. The deeds and thoughts of the peasant Ivan Ivanovich Ivanov of the village of Pokrovskoe in Siberia may have been significant in terms of history of that village, but not in terms of a history of Russia. The character and thoughts and actions of the peasant Gregory Efimovich Novykh of that same village became of great importance in terms of the history of Russia. He became notorious as Rasputin, and what Rasputin did ultimately affected not only Russia but the world.

The Ivan Ivanoviches of Russia, or the Soviet Union, are the counterparts of the John Does or the John Q. Publics of the English-speaking world: "And millions who, humble and nameless,/The straight, hard pathway plod." They are individuals, important as individuals to themselves, to their families and to their associates. To the historian, they perforce become important only when their thoughts and acts coincide with the thoughts and acts of their peers to the point of producing group attitudes or actions which affect the whole. The individuals remain anonymous to the historian, and he must depict them in very general terms.[17] It becomes a continuing challenge to make these generalizations as correct as possible. Two concepts, plus the facts which sustain them, can provide important assistance in meeting the challenge. One is the norm and value concept which has been previously discussed, the key point of which is that the majority in a group uncritically accept the norms and values of the group. There are variations. Not every person accepts every norm and value, or is affected by them; nor is acceptance uniform in intensity. This makes it necessary to proceed with caution, remembering that an "average" is an abstraction which covers a range but which may not exactly describe any individual within that range.[18]

[17] For example: Between 1906 and 1915, almost half of the twelve million peasant families resident in the forty-seven agricultural provinces of European Russia petitioned to take land from the *mir*. Slightly more than half the petitioners sought to establish family ownership; the remainder opted for individual ownership. The pattern of collectivized ownership thus persisted, although on new terms and a different scale.

The lines of poetry are from "Each in His Own Tongue," by William H. Carruth.

[18] The average weight of six men whose individual weights increase by 10 pounds from 150 to 200 is 175 pounds, a figure

The more complete and accurate the knowledge of the social norms and values, the more accurate will the generalizations be. The other concept constitutes the fifth recurrent pattern. It is the concept and pattern of the reality world, and it involves both individuals and groups.

The concept of individual and group reality worlds has already been briefly discussed, and applied as an analytical tool to the problem of subjectivity among historians and other scholars.[19] The concept may now be elaborated and applied to a broader problem. Both

---

which does not correspond to the weight of any individual in the group. An average annual rainfall of 20″ over a three-year period might mean a rainfall of 15″ in the first year, 25″ in the second, and 20″ in the third. There are also, of course, two kinds of averages—mean and median.

[19] See the discussion in the essay, "Is History a Science?" pp. 90 ff.

The concept of the reality world did not spring fully formed from any one mind. It grew out of the observations, experiments, hypotheses, and ideas of many persons; and represents a combination of experimental findings and empirical observations. One ancestral line may be traced to the research in visual perception done by Adelbert Ames and his associates. This research, originally physiological in the main, later psychological as well, centered initially on the experimental use under controlled conditions of purposeful visual illusions. The transmutation from the technical field of visual perception into the broader area of human behaviors was begun by a group of scholars at Princeton and in Hanover. Among the group were H. Cantril, W. H. Ittelson, F. P. Kilpatrick, and C. H. Bumstead.

the phrase, "reality world," and the concept which the phrase symbolizes are still sufficiently new to be unfamiliar to many, but the components which constitute the concept are readily observable and well known. The trite saying, "Different people see things differently," is, in fact, a crude description of the phenomena which the concept of the reality world seeks to explain. Its use to historians is as an analytical tool, applicable in many contexts because what it describes is a continuing or recurrent pattern in human affairs and therefore in history.

The core component of the concept of the reality world is perception, and perception, as previously noted, is very largely determined by men's multiple assumptions.[20] Perception is of many types and performs many functions. Sights, sounds, tastes, odors, and tactile impressions must be perceived as well as sensed in order to convey meaning. This also holds for intangibles and abstractions. Perception, however, is most readily described and comprehended in terms of seeing and perceiving so the discussion which follows is cast first in those terms.

Sight, which is defined by ordinary dictionaries as vision, or as the power or act of seeing, is a physiological process, more elaborate and complex than these few words suggest, but relatively simple in comparison with perception. After the eyes see an object, the brain

[20] See pp. 123 ff.

must perceive or interpret the image to make it meaningful to the beholder. The process of seeing and perceiving is virtually instantaneous and simultaneous in the case of familiar objects. We see a certain object in a certain setting and immediately perceive it to be a chair. This requires no conscious effort because we are so accustomed to doing it. Unfamiliar objects, or the distinctive details of a subspecies of an object, have to be learned. A floating object for the transportation on water of persons or things is, to casual observers, a boat. If it has sails, it is a sailboat. Those whose interests or experience have made them more knowledgeable on the subject distinguish between ships and boats; and among sloops, cutters, schooners, and other subspecies of sailboats. Both groups see the same object, but one perceives it in finer detail and with greater sophistication.

Perceiving is clearly an aspect of human life which goes on continually in all persons, often with little or no conscious thought. Despite its apparent automation, perception is really a learned activity which depends in many ways upon sophistication or the accumulation of experiences. It calls into play memories, purposes, apprehensions, value judgments, assumptions—in short, what we think we know. Individuals share certain perceptions, at least in part. The two groups mentioned above shared the perception of the floating object as a sailboat even though the second group carried the process further. But perceiving is an individual process which involves a specific person with his unique history and other personal attributes, a specific point or position in time and space, and a concrete situation. Because we all perceive all the time, whether or not we ever use that term to describe what we do, we have all learned that perceiving does not reveal absolute reality. Our perceptions are, in fact, no more than guesses based on our past experiences. These guesses constitute reality to the individual and guide his further responses.[21] There is obviously a large element of continuity in perceiving, as well as an element of change, based upon feedbacks. We stand in an always moving present, trying to translate our recollections of the past into serviceable anticipations of the future.

The process of perceiving, along with its subprocess of recollection, involves a high degree of selectivity. Humans do not respond equally nor uniformly to all stimuli. They pick and choose; they filter stimuli and recollections through the perceptive process to the point of responding only to what seems germane and important in a given situation. A friend and I once be-

[21] F. P. Kilpatrick, *Recent Transactional Perceptual Research: A Summary* (ONR Report, Princeton University, 1 May, 1955), pp. 2–4; Hadley Cantril, *The Politics of Despair* (New York: Basic Books, 1958), p. 25; Cantril and Bumstead, *op. cit.*, pp. 45–46.

came engrossed, while driving through the Marne Valley, in trying to recall the descriptions we had read of the Battles of the Marne. Printed records became so vivid that I suddenly realized that we were no longer responding to the beauties of the French countryside in spring. We were looking at the landscape, but we were perceiving terrain. We looked at church steeples and perceived observation posts; saw a stone mill at a crossroads and perceived a strong point; gazed at steep and wooded ravines and perceived difficult terrain for tanks. This was selective perception. Our particular interests and experiences temporarily made the battles of the past more real and more important than the business of sightseeing. This was a function of our particular reality worlds which, on this particular matter at least, overlapped.

Each person's reality world is formed and re-formed by his continuing transactions with persons and things around him. The transactional aspect of this is best explained by analogies. Buyers are buyers only in terms of relationship to sellers, and the converse is also true. Their shared experience is a transaction. Actors and professional lecturers sometimes speak of their audiences as having been cold or warm, that is, responsive or unresponsive. Empirical evidence demonstrates that a responsive audience evokes the best performance because a performance is a mutual, reciprocal relation or transaction. To put it another way, a transaction is an interrelationship between variables which modify each other. One of the reasons for the imprecision of studies of human behavior, including history, is that one is studying a series of transactions or interrelationships in which variables are constantly modifying each other and the relationship as well.[22]

As the individual engages in transactions he gradually learns to perceive material objects, abstractions, persons and situations in terms of how these will affect his purposes and values, and in this way constructs for himself his reality world.

> It is this psychological world which each individual in large part creates through his own experiences that determines his behavior. . . . It determines the way he sees things, what interpretations and meanings he will give to the events around him, what things he will regard as important, what significance he will attach to words, proposals, and the behavior of others in terms of his own purposes.[23]

There is continuity in a reality world, as there is in history, but a reality world is not static. It varies as

[22] A distinction is deliberately made between a transaction, which involves variables, and an interaction, which is usually thought of as taking place between two entities, one of which is an organism; the other, an objectively definable environment.

[23] Hadley Cantril and David Rodnick, *On Understanding the French Left* (Princeton: Institute for International Social Research, 1956), p. 1.

purposes change, and as aspirations and apprehensions rise or subside.[24] Its major ingredients are the assumptions which so largely determine how a person will perceive, what stimuli he will heed and what priorities he will accord them. These are obviously personal matters, and a reality world is essentially personal—the creation and possession of the individual. The uniqueness of this private world is never wholly lost, but overlappings exist among the reality worlds of those who share a common background and a common training, or common hopes, fears, purposes, and goals. Without such overlappings and similarities, there could be no empathy, and no effective communication.

There thus exist along with individual reality worlds, group reality worlds. These, also, are fluid and highly variable. Membership is motile, and there are various degrees of "belonging." If it is a group which seeks to train, or to recast its members into a common mould; that is, a group which purposefully and persistently insists upon a shared reality world, there is

[24] "Hence our reality world must undergo constant revision as we experience the inadequacies of the up-to-now assumptions we bring to the variety of new and different occasions of living. What we apparently do is to create for ourselves reality worlds which will more effectively further our basic purposes as human beings. And we do this most efficiently only if we use value satisfaction rather than consistency as our guiding standard for revision." Cantril, *Politics of Despair*, p. 25.

created an ideal type which is never fully realized but which members are constantly pressed to approach.[25] There are resemblances between the shared or group reality world and the social norms and values which the majority of a group accept. The two concepts are close, but not identical.[26] Both are tools for the analysis of group behavior, but the concept of the reality world is a more refined and sophisticated instrument. Some of the assumptions which directly influence group reality worlds are taken directly from the social norms and values of the group, but the transactions with each other and with outsiders, of those whose personal reality worlds overlap alter these assumptions in special ways. What used to be called an *esprit de corps* introduces modifications of the original assump-

[25] For an explanation of how this works among Communists see: Frank S. Meyer, *The Moulding of Communists: The Training of the Communist Cadre* (New York: Harcourt Brace, 1961), especially pp. 4, 5, 10, 11, 13. Mr. Meyer does not employ the concept of the reality world, but his discussion is highly apposite to it.

[26] It would, however, be possible to define a group and its norm and value pattern in such a way as to make it virtually identical with the reality world shared by the group. The group would have to be relatively small, very closely knit, disciplined, and specifically trained to perceive and to act in like fashion. Such a group might very well be the inner, directing core of a larger group—the cadre of a Communist Party, for example. The norm and value pattern of this inner group would, nevertheless, probably be more extensive and comprehensive, less intensive and precise than its shared reality world.

tions and also adds new ones. The two concepts, in other words, are complementary rather than interchangeable. Moreover, the existence of personal and of shared reality worlds constitutes a recurrent pattern in history while the norm and value concept is adjunct to the dichotomous patterns of change and continuity.

The sixth recurrent pattern in history, implicit in the variables which have been discussed, is the pattern of multiple causation. No generalized, single cause can adequately or accurately answer the question of why occurrences and events happened. Men are not simply material bodies in space, blindly responsive to forces which they can neither understand nor in any degree control. Neither are men purely economic beings, puppets of the mode of production or any other single determinant. It is a temptation to say with Morris Cohen, "The truth is that we cannot envisage the conduct of human beings without attributing some amount of irrationality as well as rationality to them." [27] This view provides an easy answer to those who think they have adapted to the study of human affairs the methodology of the exact physical sciences. It may seem possible to demonstrate—as Hobson did of imperialism in its heyday—that a particular course of action is, on balance, profitable only to a minority, and that support of this action by the majority is ir-

[27] Cohen, *op. cit.*, p. 121.

rational. The demonstration is specious because, like Professor Cohen's statement, it either assumes an absolute, discoverable rationality, or it ignores the question, "Rational by whose standard?" What is irrational or senseless in one reality world may be rational and sensible in another. Behaviors and attitudes which seem either incomprehensible or irrational to non-Communists, usually seem fully comprehensible and sensible when viewed from within the Communist reality world.

Is this the same as saying that men are prisoners of their reality worlds, or that "reality world" is merely another name for suprahuman forces which control men and their doings? Is there a contradiction between insisting that men are free, within limits, to make choices and are responsible for the choices they make; and saying that men's behavior is rational within the terms of their particular reality worlds? Does the admission that an act makes sense in terms of a particular reality world preclude reaching any further judgment on the action?

The answers to all these questions are qualified noes because we are dealing with variables. It is possible for men to change their assumptions, and usually they do if it is borne in upon them that the assumptions have led to faulty perceptions, erroneous actions, and undesired results. A change in major assumptions, or a major change in many lesser assumptions produces a change in the reality world. Some of those, for example, who had been perceiving and operating on the assumption that a Communist Party was the champion of all workers changed this assumption, and their political attitudes, as a result of the Soviet suppression of the Hungarian Revolt. Others did not, which reenforces the conclusion that we are dealing with variables.[28] In some, the commitment to a particular assumption, or set of assumptions, or to a particular reality world was too deep to permit a shift. This, parenthetically, is why defections by cadre, or hard-core Communists are rare. There is a point beyond which a particular choice may entail consequences which admit

28 "While I still believe that I am a good Marxist, I resigned from the Italian Communist Party as a result of the events in Hungary."—Italian high school teacher. "Yes, I have left the Party. I don't trust the Party or the Soviet Union after what happened in Hungary and in Poland."—teacher in a French technical school.

"I felt the repression of the Hungarian revolt was something necessary and horrible. I knew that drastic measures had to be taken. As soon as I understood the situation, I saw that the Soviet Union had to defend the workers of Budapest. One simply cannot question the foundations of Communism."—French worker. "I was very upset by the Hungarian affair. It literally made me sick, because it shocked me so. But I cannot leave the Party. I have been in it for 33 years."—French linotypist.

The quotations are from responses made to a survey made simultaneously in France and Italy in 1957 by the French Institute of Public Opinion and DOXA.

no feasible alternatives, a fact which is well attested by proverbs about eggs and baskets, and combustible bridges. A course of action entailing acceptance of a calculated risk of war cannot always be altered in time to avert that consequence. Full commitment to a particular position may prove to be psychologically or otherwise irreversible. The interval between the visual sighting (as opposed to electronic "sighting") and the impact of two high speed aircraft flying collision courses is so short that evasive action is impossible. As soon as one can see the other, it is already too late to avert disaster. But the causes which brought the planes together were multiple and involved many people and many things, like an enormous cable of many strands. Tracing the strands, one arrives eventually at points where choices could be and were made.[29]

The multiplicity of causes compels us in daily life

[29] As to the last question, "There must be," as Professor Berlin has observed, "a fallacy lurking somewhere in the argument of the antimoralist school." Isaiah Berlin, *Historical Inevitability* (London: Oxford University Press, 1954), p. 48.

If men should not be blamed for what they do on the ground that they can't avoid doing it, historians who praise or blame may not be faulted because they can't help themselves either. If to admit the validity of another's reality world, is to foreclose any judgment upon actions derived from it, the same attitude must be taken toward those whose reality worlds compel them to make judgments. To know all is not necessarily to forgive all. It is sometimes necessary to know a person intimately in order to dislike him.

to make at least rough evaluations of importance and relevance. We recognize the existence of distinctions —major, minor, contributory, and the like—though we may not agree as to which is which. Our categories are fuzzy, and our methods are crude. One of the best-founded criticisms of historians is that we have not sufficiently refined the methods nor devised more exact categories. Historians speak of major and minor, or primary and secondary causes; and often add, as well, time-conscious categorizations—basic, proximate, and immediate. How often have we read, and written or said, "The immediate cause was ********, but the underlying causes lay deeper." There has long been at hand in formal logic a concept which, properly employed, sometimes will help in achieving a greater degree of precision. This is the "without which," or "except for" criterion, requiring an effort to establish the cause or causes except for which the occurrence, or event, would not have happened. Unfortunately, it is more difficult to apply the criterion than to state it, and it is frequently impossible to feel certain that one has isolated the only "without which" causes. There are, of course, varying degrees of certainty.

Neither Lenin nor his Bolsheviks were an "except for" cause of the Russian Revolution of February/March, 1917. Their activities in the preceding years had helped to weaken the Imperial Government and the existing system, and had contributed to the feeling that changes for the better were possible. The same may be said with equal correctness of non-Bolshevik, non-Marxist, and non-socialist Russian reformers and revolutionaries. The February/March Revolution was an unplanned happening which took the Bolsheviks, as well as other groups, completely by surprise.[30] It is, in contrast, as certain as such matters ever can be that the Bolshevik Revolution would not have taken place in October/November, 1917 except for Lenin. It is considerably less certain that this revolution would have been entirely different, or unsuccessful without Lenin; and it is wholly uncertain that no second revolution would have taken place in Russia except for him.

It is difficult to discern all the causes of a relatively minor and simple occurrence; it is probably impossible to find all the causes of a complex, major event. There is no magic formula, no universal which encompasses all the variables and their interrelations. So far no single key has been found which will unlock all the doors leading to the past. Men have long searched for such a key, and will probably continue to do so—some from intellectual curiosity; others be-

[30] It would be inappropriate to review in these pages all the causes of the February/March Revolution, but one of the "except for" conditions was the moral and political bankruptcy of the Imperial Government which, by 1917, was unable to command respect or support even among the Tsar's own family.

cause of a desire for the power which such knowledge would bring. The search is useful or, at least, has useful by-products. Trouble begins when a searcher is able to convince himself and others that his search has been successful in discovering *the* key to human affairs, and the history of them. The value lies not in discovering *the* key, but in fashioning new keys; not in arriving at an alleged universal, but in providing additional insights which improve man's understanding of himself and of his past. This is a reciprocal process. A fuller understanding of the past produces a better comprehension of the present, and a clearer knowledge of how men think and act today suggests new methods of exploring and relating past thought and action.

An awareness that multiplicity of causes is a recurrent pattern in history, and the realization that definite answers to questions of causation are unlikely, induce a feeling of humility and stand as a constant warning against claims to have a monopoly upon truth. They require an open-mindedness, not only about new evidence but also about new methods of analysis. The complexity and the difficulty of the problem is a standing challenge to the skills, the ingenuity, the knowledge, and the intellectual integrity of the historian. The best he can offer will not be good enough, but nothing less than his best will serve at all.